BUS REVIEW 16

Review of 2000 by **Stewart J Brown**

Above: Warwickshire County Council took the unusual step of buying its own buses for use on tendered services - and the buses themselves were unusual too, being Mercedes-Benz Citaros. They carry the county's Countylinks livery and are operated under contract by Guide Friday and Johnsons of Henley-in-Arden. The use of two-and-three seating increases the seating capacity to 48 - 10 more than the Citaros in the First Manchester fleet.

Front cover: Leon Motor Services of Finningley took its first new double-deckers for 20 years with the delivery of two Dennis Tridents with East Lancs Lolyne bodies. The company's last new double-decker, in 1980, was an Alexander-bodied Fleetline.
David Barrow

Back cover, upper: After buying only single-deckers for most of the 1990s, Travel West Midlands showed renewed interest in double-deckers, taking 102 Volvo B7TLs with Plaxton President bodies in 1999-2000. Most were 74-seaters.

Back cover, lower: Blue Bus of Horwich is a regular buyer of new buses and its 2000 intake included a Volvo B10BLE with Wright Renown body, seen here prior to entering service on one of the company's Bolton routes.

Contents

Introduction 3
New in Scotland 4
TransBus unites Britain's biggest bus builders...........6
Artic expansion in FirstGroup operations 9
Scania delivers last UK 'deckers 13
2000 round-up 14
Continued growth at Arriva 18
Volvo launches B10M replacement 21
London's year of the 'decker 22
Who makes what? 26
Bodybuilders active in the UK 28
Coaching contrasts 29
New in the Midlands 30

All change at Stagecoach 32
Dennis expands coach range 35
Optare passes to US ownership....................................36
New in the North West 38
Who owns whom... 40
Wright joins the double-deck fray 42
New in the North East and Yorkshire 43
The school run..44
Web index 45
The end of the Olympian 46
Deliveries 2000 47
Forward orders 48

All of the big groups have stopped buying Mercedes-Benz Vario minibuses. Arriva has chosen Mini Pointer Darts for routes which might in the past have been allocated Varios, while FirstGroup has chosen the Optare Solo. Among the Solo deliveries in 2000 were some for PMT, trading here as First Crosville.

First published 2001
ISBN 0–946265–34–8
© Bus Enthusiast Publishing Company, 2001
Typeset in Times and Helvetica
Electronic page makeup by Jeremy Scott
Printed by Pillans & Wilson, Edinburgh

Published by
Bus Enthusiast Publishing Company
5 Hallcroft Close,
Ratho, Newbridge
Midlothian EH28 8SD
Tel/fax: 0131 333 2796
www.busenthusiast.com
Bus Enthusiast is an imprint of
Arthur Southern Ltd.

Introduction

THE YEAR 2000 could prove to be a turning point for British bus manufacturing, with the union of the country's three biggest bus builders in TransBus International. TransBus unites Alexander, Plaxton and Dennis - and creates what is one of Europe's biggest bus makers. The ramifications are not immediately clear, but watch for new alignments between the chassis and body makers outside TransBus, for rationalisation of production facilities within TransBus and - hopefully - for new export sales for all three partners.

Among operators the big changes were in London, with Metroline being bought by the owners of Singapore Bus Services, and London Buses re-establishing itself as a bus operator to rescue the failed Harris Bus operation which had called in the receivers at the end of 1999.

London orders helped boost double-deck deliveries in 2000, and large numbers of new low-floor deckers were delivered to all of the big London fleets. There was also a resurgence of interest in double-deckers among smaller operators and buyers included Manchester area companies Bullock, Dennis's, Finglands, JP Travel and Mayne, and, in Yorkshire, Leon. A number of independents also took advantage of Scania's surfeit of stock-build Cityzens to add new double-deckers to their fleets.

There were some striking new designs on the streets of Britain in 2001 - the East Lancs Myllennium, the articulated Wright Eclipse Fusion and the Mercedes-Benz Citaro. Plaxton promised a new model - Bus 2000 - but that was put on hold when the TransBus proposals were made public. Also on hold was the Irisbus/Renault Agora Line which was to have been bodied by Optare. This was because the future ownership of Irisbus was caught up in the ramifications of Volvo's aborted take-over bid for Scania which had led to Volvo buying Renault's commercial vehicle business which in turn was a part-owner of Irisbus.

Yes, it is complicated.

Dennis once again was the leading supplier of new buses to UK operators, delivering almost 1,500 against Volvo's figure of just under 1,000.

In coaching, most new Plaxton coaches in 2000 were old coaches - insofar as they were Premieres, Excaliburs and Primas, rather than Panthers and Paragons. But after a slow start, the new models started to appear in the late spring and by the end of the year there were around 130 on the road. The new range is wider, at 2.55m against the old legal maximum of 2.5m, and benefits from a stainless-steel frame and multiplex wiring.

Volvo, as usual, sold more coaches than anybody else. It delivered 360 coaches in 2000, according to the Society of Motor Manufacturers and Traders, where no other manufacturer sold more than 100 full-sized coaches. The Dennis Javelin used to be number two in the sales league table, but in 2000 had fallen to sixth place behind Iveco, Scania, Bova and DAF. The company must be hoping that the rear-engined R-series will revive its fortunes in the coach market.

As always, I pay tribute to the work of the PSV Circle and its members who assiduously record the intricate goings on in operators' fleets throughout the British Isles. To keep up-to-date with the ever-changing scene read *Buses* every month, and if you want to know who's running what, the Bus Handbooks produced by British Bus Publishing provide detailed fleet lists for all of the better-known (and many lesser-known) fleets in Britain and Ireland.

Stewart J Brown
Reedley Hallows, 2001

The first of Plaxton's new-generation coaches for an English operator was this Paragon for Battersby Silver Grey of Morecambe. (The very first of the new models went to Park's of Hamilton.) Based on a Volvo B10M chassis it is in the livery of Leger Holidays, a tour company which uses dedicated coaches hired in from a wide range of operators.

New in Scotland

Outwardly indistinguishable from the large number of Plaxton-bodied Dennis Tridents in service with Lothian Buses, this is in fact one of six Volvo B7TLs purchased for evaluation. It acquired a West Midlands registration after entering service because of some confusion over chassis numbers. *John Burnett*

The first purpose-built permanent open-toppers for a UK fleet for more than 60 years were four Plaxton-bodied Dennis Tridents for Lothian Buses. *Gavin Booth*

The Volvo/Van Hool combination has long been popular with Scottish coach operators. This B10M was delivered to Docherty's Midland Coaches of Auchterarder early in the year.

Caetano's old-style Compass body, a design inherited with the UVG business in 1998, has been phased out of production in favour of the new Nimbus. The last few Compasses were delivered in 2000, all on Dennis Dart chassis, and buyers included Dart Buses of Paisley.

Waverley Travel has expanded operation of tendered routes in Edinburgh. A modern fleet of Mercedes Varios and, as here, Dennis Mini Pointer Darts is used. *John Burnett*

TransBus unites Britain's biggest bus builders

IT IS THE start of the biggest shake-up in British bus and coach manufacturing since Volvo acquired Leyland Bus in 1987. TransBus International is the name of the new company which is uniting the British manufacturing interests of Mayflower and Henlys. The surprise deal was announced in August, and was cleared by the Department of Trade and Industry in December. Ownership of TransBus is split 70:30 between Mayflower and Henlys.

Mayflower's contribution to TransBus is Alexander and Dennis, plus specialist body kit manufacturer Metsec. Henlys' contribution is Plaxton and coach dealer Kirkby. There is significant overlap in the Alexander and Plaxton bus body ranges as the table on page 8 shows. Indeed for UK operators the only area in which they do not compete directly is 12m single-deckers, where Alexander build the ALX300 and Plaxton is not represented since it ceased building Prestiges in 1999. Plaxton and Alexander were the two biggest bodybuilders in Britain before the merger - now they dwarf the remaining mainstream builders, Wright, Optare and East Lancs.

Significantly the TransBus deal excludes the US operations of both groups - the merger is primarily a UK affair.

Alexander has two manufacturing plants, at Falkirk and Belfast, and has been owned by Mayflower since 1995. Plaxton has three locations. The biggest is in Scarborough, the company's home town, where it builds the extremely successful Pointer 2 bus and all of the full-size coach models. Then comes Plaxton Wigan. This was

Northern Counties until the end of 1998 and had been owned by Henlys since 1995. The smallest of Henlys' manufacturing facilities is at Anston, near Sheffield, where the Small Bus Division produces the Beaver 2 bus and Cheetah coach on the Mercedes-Benz Vario chassis. Henlys also has a design centre in Hungary which is part of the TransBus operation.

Dennis builds chassis at Guildford in a modern plant on the edge of the town. Dennis has significant export business, particularly in the Far East where it has long been one of the major suppliers to Hong Kong fleets. The same can be said of Alexander. And both Dennis and Alexander have established a manufacturing base in the USA: Thomas Dennis. Plaxton does relatively little in the way of export sales - other than coaches to Eire. But it has had some success selling Pointer 2s in Canada.

The unification of Alexander, Dennis and Plaxton follows a fierce battle in 1998, when Henlys and Dennis announced a merger - a plan which was scuppered when Mayflower sailed in, bought Dennis, and left Plaxton high and dry.

Concerned about the long-term implications of the Dennis-Alexander link, Plaxton had been developing a new integral - coded Bus 2000 - to challenge the Dart SLF. Plaxton was, of course, heavily dependant on Dennis to support production of its Pointer 2 range. Bus 2000 was to have been launched in the autumn of 2000 and promised new style - but the project was axed as soon as TransBus was announced. The appearance of a Plaxton integral bus now seems unlikely, but it will be interesting to see if the new body structure is developed further - perhaps as a successor to the Pointer 2 and the ALX200.

Quite what will happen next is difficult to forecast. The general opinion is that with over-capacity in the UK bus-building industry there will be at least one plant closure at TransBus. There also has to be some rationalisation in the range of bus bodies built by Alexander and Plaxton, although that clearly won't happen overnight. Alexander's ALX100 minibus wouldn't be missed, but the ALX200 and the Pointer 2 are both strong sellers. And the same applies to the President and ALX400.

One of the most successful products of the TransBus partners is the Dennis Dart with Plaxton Pointer bodywork. This is the shortest version - the 8.8m Mini Pointer Dart - in operation with Elcock Reisen of Telford. The Mini Pointer Dart has been bought by many operators who would in the past have chosen a Mercedes minibus.

History shows that when major mergers take place in the UK the new combined company always sells fewer vehicles than its two constituents did on their own. Operators who dual-sourced as a matter of policy, or who alternated between Alexander and Plaxton, will clearly have to look elsewhere if they want to maintain such a policy. So while TransBus International is big, its very existence may well open up new opportunities for the other bodybuilders.

The new scenario also may cause some discomfort among other chassis builders, and could lead to them strengthening their relationships with the "independents" - East Lancs and Wright. Equally, a significant proportion of East Lancs' output has been on Dennis chassis, although the appearance of the Vyking on the Volvo B7TL during the year shows that this could be about to change. Ironically, East Lancs was instrumental in helping Dennis to get established in the bus market in the late 1970s, in part because the company was worried about the long-term availability of Leyland chassis following the launch of the integral Titan and saw Dennis as a way of reducing its dependence on Leyland.

Wright already has strong relationships with DAF, Scania and Volvo, and is building very few bodies on Dennis chassis. Indeed no Wright-bodied Dennises were produced in 2000.

Outside the UK Henlys retains control of US builder Blue Bird, and its share in Prevost and NovaBus, which are both jointly-owned with Volvo. Similarly, Mayflower retains its interest in Thomas Dennis, which came on stream in 2000 as a builder of the Thomas SLF200, an Alexander-bodied Dart for the US market.

TransBus is the fourth-largest bus and coach manufacturer in Europe after EvoBus, Volvo and Irisbus. It has the ability to build around 2,500 chassis and 3,500 bodies annually.

TransBus brings together the manufacturers of Britain's two best-selling double-deck bodies, Alexander and Plaxton. Before the merger, London United was buying from both builders and in 2000 took ALX400s (above) and Presidents (below) on Volvo B7TL chassis. The ALX400 is at Heathrow Airport; the President at Hounslow bus station.

TransBus hopes to secure more export sales. Among the more unusual deliveries in 2000 by two of its consituents were two Plaxton-bodied Dennis Dart SLFs for Hagvagnar of Reykjavik in Iceland. To cope with the rigours of Icelandic winters they had double glazing and Webasto oil-fired auxiliary heaters. These were the first Dennis buses ever for operation in Iceland.

Plaxton was for many years primarily a builder of coaches rather than buses. It remains the biggest supplier of coaches to UK fleets, but coach production has now been overtaken by buses. During 2000 the first examples of its new Paragon and Panther models entered service, and included this Paragon on a Volvo B10M chassis for Wallace Arnold.

THE TRANSBUS INTERNATIONAL PRODUCT RANGE

Body	Type	Chassis availability
Alexander ALX100	minibus	Mercedes Vario
Plaxton Beaver 2	minibus	Mercedes Vario
Plaxton Cheetah	minicoach	Mercedes Vario
Alexander ALX200	single-deck	Dennis Dart SLF
Plaxton Pointer 2	single-deck	Dennis Dart SLF
Alexander ALX300	12m single-deck	DAF SB220, MAN 18.220, Volvo B10BLE
Alexander ALX400	double-deck	DAF DB250, Dennis Trident, Volvo B7TL
Plaxton President	double-deck	DAF DB250, Dennis Trident, Volvo B7TL
Alexander ALX500	12m double-deck	Dennis Trident 3-axle, Volvo Super Olympian
Metsec	12m double-deck	Dennis Trident 3-axle, Volvo Super Olympian
Plaxton Prima	coach	DAF SB3000, Dennis Javelin, Volvo B7R
Plaxton Premiere	coach	DAF SB3000, Dennis Javelin, Volvo B10M
Plaxton Excalibur	coach	Dennis Javelin, Volvo B10M, B12M
Plaxton Paragon	coach	Dennis R, Iveco EuroRider,Volvo B10M, B12M
Plaxton Panther	coach	Dennis R, Iveco EuroRider,Volvo B10M, B12M

Chassis	Type	UK body availability
Dennis Dart SLF	midibus	Alexander, Caetano, East Lancs, Marshall, Plaxton, Wright
Dennis Javelin	mid-engined coach	Berkhof, Caetano, Marcopolo, Plaxton
Dennis R-series	rear-engined coach	Berkhof, Plaxton
Dennis Trident	2-axle double-deck	Alexander, East Lancs, Plaxton
Dennis Trident	3-axle double-deck	export only

Artic expansion in FirstGroup operations

THERE WERE no significant changes in the structure of FirstGroup's UK bus operations in 2000, although there was considerable interest in the new vehicles it was buying. Indeed the only noteworthy territorial change saw the group abandon its Fife First operation in July, set up in June 1997 to compete with Stagecoach in Dunfermline and between the Dunfermline area and Edinburgh.

Overseas there was one significant piece of retrenchment, with FirstGroup selling its 26 per cent interest in New World First Bus in May. The operation in Hong Kong had been set up 18 months earlier. However the Hong Kong link did have an unusual side effect, with the arrival at First Pennine in November of 10 three-axle Leyland Olympians from New World First Bus for operation on schools services. They had Alexander bodies and dated from 1993.

A small-scale acquisition in January saw First York acquire York Pullman's Easylink bus operations from Durham Travel Services, with seven Dennis Darts and two open-top 'deckers. York Pullman had been owned by DTS since 1993. Its previous owner was Kingston-upon-Hull City Transport.

Following the success of its high-frequency Overground services, launched in Glasgow in August 1999, FirstGroup introduced the Overground concept to Edinburgh, Bradford and Sheffield in the summer. This was followed in September by the Leicester Metro - a scaled-down Overground tailored to the needs of smaller cities. With the new image came the withdrawal of all 33 of First Leicester's Renault minibuses. They were replaced by Mercedes and Volvo B6s transferred from other group companies. To coincide with the launch of Leicester Metro, First Leicester adopted a new white, green and yellow livery. This replaced the previous GRT-style cream and two-tone red, and a short-lived experimental red and blue scheme which had been applied to around a dozen buses.

FirstGroup showed an interest in two rather different types of bus in 2000, neither of which was used in passenger service. First, in August, it unveiled a low-cost Blue Bird school bus. Built in the USA by a subsidiary of Henlys, the front-engined TC had a three-step entrance, 61 seats and no fewer than 14 side windows - on each side. Although right-hand-drive, the prototype was not certified for UK operation. FirstGroup believes that purpose-built school buses may have a role to play in its British operations, hence its interest in the rather basic Blue Bird.

Then in October the group evaluated a 15m-long three-axle left-hand-drive Mercedes-Benz Citaro. This was examined by FirstGroup managers and staff at locations around the country. It reportedly offered no problems in urban traffic - but did come to grief in a bus depot somewhere in the north of England…

The 15m bus could carry up to 135 people, but offered just 44 seats. Buses of this length are not, as yet, legal in the UK but they could offer a lower-cost alternative to the articulated vehicles which FirstGroup was buying in 2000.

There were some changes at First Manchester which became responsible for the 50-bus First Pennine operation. This had previously been run by First PMT. The company had been set up as

Perhaps the most striking buses in UK operation are the new Wright-bodied Volvo B7LA artics delivered to FirstGroup in 2000. The first entered service with First Bradford as part of the launch of Overground, which marked a major improvement to the city's bus network.

The new Mercedes-Benz Citaro made a big impact in the First Manchester fleet, with 60 being allocated to the company's Oldham depot. Citaros were also delivered to Bus Eireann, and to two Warwickshire independents who were operating them on tendered services on behalf of the county council. *David Barrow*

Wright was a major supplier to FirstGroup in 2000, providing bodies on Volvo B6BLE, B7LA, B10BLE and Scania L94. The B6BLEs were for fleets in the south of England and had Crusader II bodies. This one is with First Bristol.

First Glasgow took new Scanias and Volvos in 2000. The Volvos were B10BLEs with Alexander ALX300 bodies. There were 30.

Pennine Blue in 1990 and was bought by PMT in 1993, at which time it ran around 30 buses. First Manchester at the end of the year took over the bus operations of Coachmasters of Rochdale, which had started in September 1999. The company, run by bus dealer Houston Ramm, was mainly involved in school services but also operated between Rochdale and Wigan. It ran 19 buses.

Another acquisition at the end of the year saw FirstGroup's North American interests expand with the purchase of Canadian school bus operator Hertz Group. This runs 735 buses in Saskatchewan.

FirstGroup's activities in Yorkshire attracted the attention of the Office of Fair Trading which in October raided offices of both FirstGroup and Arriva as part of an enquiry into operations in the Leeds area. Quite what the OFT suspected had not been made public by the end of the year.

In the London area the two companies which traded as First Capital - Capital Citybus and Walthamstow Citybus - were re-named in April, becoming First Capital East and First Capital North respectively.

There were some exciting new buses for FirstGroup in 2000, including most of an order for 37 articulated Volvo B7LAs with Wright's impressive Eclipse Fusion body, which had been unveiled at Coach & Bus 99. The vehicles were to be shared between Aberdeen (six), Bradford (11), Leeds (two) and Hampshire (18). The first entered service in Bradford in the summer.

However FirstGroup's interest in artics was not entirely at the expense of double-deckers, and well over 100 Volvo B7TLs with Alexander ALX400 bodies were delivered to its fleets in Aberdeen, Bradford, Bristol, Hampshire, Leeds and Leicester. A small number of Dennis Tridents with East Lancs Lolyne bodies joined the First Bristol and First Western National fleets.

In London the group took one B7TL demonstrator with East Lancs Vyking body, which was operated by CentreWest. It also took Dennis Tridents with both Alexander ALX400 and Plaxton President bodies, for First Capital and First CentreWest respectively.

Single-deckers were mainly Volvo B6BLE and B10BLE with Wright bodies, but in Manchester a fleet of 60 Mercedes-Benz Citaros entered service at Oldham, significantly reducing the number of Atlanteans operating for First Manchester. These were the first examples of Mercedes' new citybus for UK service. Scanias with Wright bodies went to Eastern Counties, Manchester and Glasgow. Around 150 Dennis Dart SLFs, with bodies by Marshall (for London), Alexander and Plaxton were also delivered. Small buses included a few Mini Pointer Darts (at First Beeline and First Midland Red), and around 50 Optare Solos with First Bradford, First PMT and First Western National being the main users.

Noteworthy departures were the last Seddon Pennine VIIs from First Edinburgh in August.

While fleet replacement had continued at a reasonable level in 2000, no major orders were announced by FirstGroup for delivery in 2001.

Underlining FirstGroup's primary role as an operator of buses rather than coaches, the only new coaches purchased in 2000 were four Volvo B10Ms with Plaxton Expressliner bodies. These joined the First Wessex National fleet and were for use on Flightlink contracts.

In Bristol, new Dennis Tridents with East Lancs Lolyne bodies were introduced to the city's park-and-ride services. East Lancs has not in the past been a major supplier to FirstGroup.

New double-deckers entered service in significant numbers with FirstGroup provincial fleets in Hampshire, Bristol, Leicester and Yorkshire. Most were Volvo B7TLs with Alexander ALX400 bodies, as seen here with First Leeds. *David Barrow*

Seen before being delivered to First CentreWest is a Volvo B7TL with East Lancs Vyking body, which was to spend six months demonstrating to FirstGroup in London. *David Barrow*

Apart from double-deckers for CentreWest, Plaxton did relatively little business with FirstGroup in 2000. It supplied three Mini Pointer Darts to First Bee Line for operation in the Maidenhead area. One is seen outside Windsor Castle.

FIRSTGROUP SUBSIDIARIES AND PRINCIPAL TRADING NAMES

CentreWest London Buses
  First Challenger
  First Ealing Buses
  First Gold Arrow
  First London Buslines
  First Orpington Buses
  First Uxbridge Buses
  Heathrow Fast
Essex Buses
  Airport Buses
  First Eastern National
  First Phoenix
  First Thamesway
First Aberdeen
  Kirkpatrick of Deeside
  Mairs of Aberdeen
First Beeline
First Bristol Buses
  First Badgerline
  First CityLine
  First Dorchester
  First Durbins
  First Southern National
  First Streamline
First Capital East
First Capital North
First Cymru Buses
  First Brewers

First SWT
First Eastern Counties Omnibus
  First Blue Bus
  Halesworth Transit
   Flying Banana
  Rosemary Coaches
First Edinburgh
First Glasgow (No1)
First Glasgow (No2)
  First Ayrshire
First Hampshire
  First Provincial Buses
  First Southampton
First Manchester
  First Pennine
  First Pioneer Bus
   First Rochdale
First Midland Red Buses
First Wessex National
First Western National Buses
  North Devon
  First Red Bus
Leicester Citybus
  First Leicester
Mainline Group
  First Mainline
Midland Bluebird
  First Edinburgh

Northampton Transport
  First Northampton
PMT
  First Crosville
  First PMT
  Red Rider
Rider York
  First York
Yorkshire Rider
  First Bradford
  First Calderline
  First Huddersfield
  First Leeds
  First Superbus
  First Quickstep

Overseas operations
First Student (USA)
First Transit (USA)

Rail operations
First Great Eastern
First Great Western
First North Western
Tramlink (Croydon) (20%)

Scania delivers last UK 'deckers

SCANIA WITHDREW from the double-deck bus business in 2000, with the delivery of the last of a batch of 30 N113s with East Lancs Cityzen bodies which had been built speculatively in 1999, primarily with an eye to London sales - a ploy frustrated by London's quick switch to low-floor models. These went to a variety of small operators and the last was delivered to Hardings of Liverpool in October.

Scania's first involvement with double-deckers was in a joint project with Metro-Cammell, the Metropolitan, which was produced between 1973 and 1978. This offered outstanding performance, but at the cost of poor fuel consumption. The body structure was prone to rusting, and many Metropolitans lasted just seven years being withdrawn when their initial Certificate of Fitness expired.

However Scania saw a future in double-deckers, and in 1981 launched its N112 chassis. Like the Metropolitan before it, this used a transverse 11-litre Scania engine, driving through a Scania automatic gearbox. The gearbox would prove to be a frequent source of complaint, with failures commonplace. Ultimately Scania would offer proprietary gearboxes from Voith.

Double-deck bodywork on Scanias was initially built by Alexander, East Lancs, Marshall and Northern Counties. The N112 metamorphosed into the N113 in 1988, the change bringing some specification improvements including more power.

Annual sales were, at best, in double figures. The model got off to a slow start, and by 1986 double-deck bus sales totalled just 50. London Buses with two sizeable batches in 1991-92 - 20 with Alexander bodies and 42 bodied by Northern Counties - marked the finest hour for Scania's N113. Some stock-build N113s were also bought by London. Other London area operators were BTS Coaches, Grey-Green and Kentish Bus.

Municipal buyers included Hull, Nottingham and Newport (each of which also ran Scania single-deckers) plus Cardiff. Scania made no real impact on Passenger Transport Executive fleets. Tyne & Wear bought two early examples with Alexander bodies, but the privatised former PTE fleets did show some interest. West Midlands Travel took 40 with Alexander bodies in 1990. Ten joined the Yorkshire Rider fleet in 1990, to be followed by 32 in 1991. Other former PTE fleets buying Scania 'deckers in 1991 were Busways (10) and GM Buses (five).

Among the more significant independent buyers were Mayne of Manchester and Liverline of Liverpool. British Bus subsidiaries Midland Fox took 20 with East Lancs bodies in 1994, followed by Derby City Transport and Midland Red North with five each in 1995.

In 1995 Scania worked with East Lancs to produce the Cityzen, with a style - from John Worker Design - which was radically different from anything else East Lancs had built. This was initially bought by Northumbria, which took the first 13, and later by Brighton & Hove. Cityzens were also bought by a number of independents including Bluebird and Mayne in Manchester, and Dunn-Line in

Nottingham. The only buyer of a new Scania double-decker in Scotland was A1 Service.

Perhaps the most unusual Scania double-deck buses were two 11.2m-long East Lancs-bodied 92-seaters, based on the K92 model with an in-line rear engine. These were built for Boro'Line Maidstone in 1987.

The move to low-floor double-deckers has left Scania without a suitable product for the UK market - for the time being at least - but in 2001 it will be launching an articulated single-decker, the L94UA. This will build on the company's growing strength in the supply of 12m-long single-deckers, with both Arriva and FirstGroup having bought significant numbers of these in the late 1990s and into 2000.

The 18m-long L94UA, with bodywork by Wrights, was to be launched early in 2001.

The last Scania double-deckers entered service in 2000, being N113s with East Lancs Cityzen bodies which had been built as stock vehicles. This one joined the fleet of Bullock of Cheadle, a company which had the distinction of being unique in putting into service step-entrance and low-floor double-deckers with consecutive registrations. This is W675PTD. W674PTD is a low-floor Dennis - see page 39. *David Barrow*

2000 round-up

January

• Johnsons of Worksop buys Redfern Coaches of Mansfield (12 vehicles).

• Durham Travel Services sells its York Pullman bus operations to FirstGroup, with seven Darts and two open-top 'deckers. York Pullman was bought by DTS from Kingston-upon-Hull City Transport in 1993.

• Bova delivers its 5,000th Europa. It goes to an Italian company.

• Lothian Region Transport is renamed Lothian Buses.

• Northern Blue, which started running services in competition with Blackburn Transport in November 1999, withdraws from commercial operation to concentrate on contracted work.

• Shamrock Travel of Pontypridd buys Venture Travel of Cardiff (16 vehicles, 10 of which are 20 years old).

• Angloblue Coaches of Leeds ceases operations. It operated local bus services in Leeds in the early 1990s, which it sold to Yorkshire Rider in 1996. At the same time it took over Yorkshire Rider's Gold Rider coaching business.

• The New Edinburgh Tramway Co claims to be on the verge of signing a deal to finance the construction of a £35million system linking Edinburgh and Leith - but little more is heard of it.

February

• MAN buys ERF. The Cheshire manufacturer had previously been owned by Canadian builder Western Star. The acquisition brings an end to ERF's plans to enter the UK bus market with a low-floor minibus - the company had in 1999 acquired the rights to manufacture the ill-fated Marshall Minibus design.

• National Express subsidiary AirLinks buys the London United Airbus operation, with 19 Volvo Olympian double-deck coaches and also takes over the Brighton operations of Skills of Nottingham, alomg with eight coaches.

• Metroline is bought by Singapore-based DelGro, owners of Singapore Bus Services, in a deal worth £74million. The man from DelGro, he say yes.

March

• The European Commission blocks the planned takeover of Scania by Volvo.

• The Oxford Bus Company drops the Citylink name for its express services and rebrands them as Oxford Express. The Citylink name dated back to when the company was part of the National Bus Company.

• Cummins announces new ISB and ISC engines to replace the B- and C-series. The new engines meet Euro 3 emission requirements which come in to force in October 2001.

• Stagecoach sells Porterbrook, the railway rolling stock leasing company. It had owned the company since 1996.

• Motor Coach Industries of Macedonia advertises its intention to sell in the UK, with a range of minibuses, full-size buses and coaches. None appear in 2000.

• Plaxton reveals that it is developing a new model, Bus 2000, for launch in the autumn.

April

• Trent is to sell all 41 of its Optare MetroRiders, with 20 going to Wilts & Dorset and 21 to Yorkshire Traction. They are being replaced by new low-floor Solos and Excels.

• London Frog launches amphibious tours of the capital using DUKWs.

• Universal of Chadderton closes. The operation had started in September 1997 and had built up to a fleet of 20 vehicles. Some of its services are taken over by Stagecoach Manchester.

• Toyota launches new-look Optimo V. Like the Mark IV, it is built in two widths - 2.12m and 2.29m. The engine is unchanged - a 4.1-litre Toyota four-cylinder diesel, but it now has a six-speed gearbox.

• AirLinks, part of the National Express Group, buys Capital Logistics. Capital had been owned by Tellings Golden Miller which retains its three LT routes - the 726, H26 and U3. The deal adds 71 vehicles to the AirLinks fleet.

• The first examples of Volvo's B7LA - A for Articulated - with Wright's new Eclipse Fusion body enter service with First Bradford. Industry magazine *Coach and Bus Week* headlines their arrival: "Britain's best bus?".

• Volkswagen takes an 18.7 per cen shareholding in Scania.

• The Optare Solo wins the Queens Award for Innovation. Over 500, worth £35million, have been sold - that's an average of £70,000 each.

• Anglo-American Coach Industries, the Ayats importer, take a stake in Macedonian builder MCI and announces that it will be importing MCI coaches to the UK. None appear in 2000. Will they ever?

• A Neoplan Starliner operated by Perrys of Cheslyn Hay is coach of the year at the 2000 Brighton Coacl Rally.

• Volvo announces that it is buying Renault VI and the associated Mack trucks business.

• Stagecoach Fife Buses buys Alisons of Dunfermline (30 very old vehicles).

May

• The Opus, a joint project between Wright of Ballymena and US builder Chance Coach is unveiled at a trade show in Houston, Texas. The 9.1m-long low-floor bus has been developed by Wright Expotech for the US market. The body resembles Wright's new Solar and Eclipse and in two-door form has 24 seats and room for 25 standees. The Chance chassis uses a Cummins ISB engine and Allison B300R gearbox.

• The first Spanish-built OVI Versatile coach for a British fleet is delivered to Bibby's of Ingleton. It is based on a DAF SB3000 chassis. OVI stands for Omnibus Vehiculos Industriales and produces bodies in a factory previously used by Obradors, a builder which closed in 1996.

• Croydon Tramlink opens. It is operated by FirstGroup with a fleet of 24 Bombardier trams.

• Stagecoach Bluebird buys JW Coaches of Banchory (13 vehicles). It retains the JW name.

• First Berkhof Axial 100 double-deck for the UK is delivered to Siesta International. It is based on a Scania K124.

• Autobus, manufacturer of the Nouvelle midicoach, is renamed Optare Rotherham. It has been owned by Optare since 1996.

June

• The new Thomas Dennis factory opens in Jamestown, North Carolina. It is building the Thomas SLF200 - a Dennis Dart SLF with Alexander ALX200 for the North American market. The first 65 Thomas SLF200s were built in Britain, but the opening of the new factory allows the assembly of CKD kits and an increase in local content. Early orders include 11 for Bryce Canyon National Park in Utah, to be operated by Lewis Brothers Stages, and 35 for the City of Albuquerqe Transit.

• Transdev, owner of London United, takes an 18 per cent share of Nottingham City Transport.

• French operator Cars Cariane takes a 20 per cent stake in council-owned Eastbourne Buses. Cariane is a subsidiary of France's state-owned railway company, SNCF.

• Eddie Brown Tours buys Wrays of Harrogate. Wrays operate 16 coaches and the take-over swells the Eddie Brown fleet to 45.

• Venture Travel (owned by Shamrock Travel) buys Stevens Travel of Newport.

• Houston Ramm, the Rochdale-based dealer and operator of the Coachmaster fleet, acquires Williams (Bala) which operates 15 vehicles.

• Holmeswood Coaches buys Walkers of Anderton (22 vehicles). The Holmeswood fleet now numbers 115.

July

• AW Group, the dealer handling UK sales of Irisbus coaches and Blue Bird buses, is renamed Coach Europe. It then announces that it will be selling Iveco EuroRiders with Plaxton bodywork in 2001. Twenty are to be built. Previously the EuroRider had only been available in the UK with Beulas coachwork.

• St Andrew Square bus station in Edinburgh - opened in 1957 - is closed for major redevelopment of the site, with a new bus station to open towards the end of 2002. Services use nearby street stands, most of which are in St Andrew Square and Waterloo Place.

• The operations of Newmark Coaches of Stratford become part of the Status Group and are reconstituted as Stratford Blue Travel.

• London Traveller closes its five-vehicle St Albans operation.

• The last Volvo Olympian for a UK fleet enters service with Yorkshire Coastliner.

• Springfield Coachways of Wigan has its operating licence revoked after breaking drivers hours regulations and using vehicles on service which did not have valid test certificates. The company had authorisation to run 16 buses. Its services are taken over (in August) by First Manchester and South Lancs Transport.

• MAN announces that it is considering selling the Turkish-built Lion's Coach in the UK - but not before 2002.

In July Springfield Coachways of Wigan had its licence revoked. Its fleet had included Mini Pointer Darts.

The Londoners, part of the Status Group, closed down in the summer. Its last new coaches were four Volvo B7Rs with air-conditioned Plaxton Prima bodies, delivered in Status Group's corporate livery layout.

• Operation of Routemasters by Reading Mainline ceases. The operation had started in July 1994 and had been taken over by Reading Transport in 1998. The Routemasters are replaced by ex-Cardiff Optare Excels.

• Volvo Coach Sales announce that in 2001 the B7R will be available with Jonckheere bodywork in the UK. Since its launch in 1997 it has been sold exclusively with Plaxton's Prima body.

• Plaxton announces 50 redundancies at its Wigan plant - formerly known as Northern Counties.

• The Londoners (22 coaches) closes down and calls in the receivers. It was part of the Status Group.

• Coach dealer Moseley Distributors announces that it has acquired a minority stake in Long's Coaches of Salsburgh. Long's run 10 vehicles.

• East Lancs unveils its Vyking body on the Volvo B7TL chassis. The first is a 10.2m-long two-door bus to FirstGroup's London specification, with 63 seats and two doors. It enters trial service with First CentreWest.

• What are expected to be the last Optare MetroRiders to be built are delivered to Shamrock of Pontypridd.

• MC travel of Melksham closes (12 vehicles).

August

• The Bath Bus Company buys three of the Leyland-DAB artics which had been operating in Sheffield, originally with the South Yorkshire PTE and latterly with First Mainline.

• DaimlerChrysler buys Western Star whose products include Orion buses, produced in the USA and Canada.

• Moseley PCV announce that it is to sell the Sitcar Beluga in the UK, based on the Mercedes O815 front-engined light truck chassis. Sitcar is an Italian builder and the Beluga seats 27. Moseley plans to sell 30 in 2000-2001. The Mercedes O815 has a 152bhp OM904LA engine and a ZF 5S-42 gearbox.

• National Express buys US operator School Services & Leasing, which operates 3,100 buses.

Border Buses was sold in August to Northern Blue. The fleet had included MCW Metrobuses, such as this one-time West Midlands PTE example. Its new owners introduced second-hand Dominators to the fleet.

• Merseytravel announces plans for a light rapid transit system for Liverpool with three lines to serve Kirkby, Prescott and south Liverpool.

• Northern Blue buys Border Buses and the associated Viscount Central coach business, with some 16 vehicles in total. At their peak in mid-1999 Border and Viscount ran 60 vehicles between them.

• Limebourne Travel buys Travel London from National Express, including the company's 27 Optares

• Manchester Metrolink secures funding for extensions to Rochdale, Wythenshawe and Ashton-under-Lyne.

• Edwards Coaches of South Wales (65 vehicles) calls in the receivers - but is for sale as a going concern.

• Go-Ahead Group rejects a take-over bid by a French consortium.

• National Express buys Prism Rail, with four franchises: Cardiff Railways, Wales and West, West Anglia Great Northern and c2c.

September

• MAN buys Neoplan.

• Stagecoach buys the bus operations of Phil Anslow of Pontypool, with 28 vehicles. Phil Anslow continues running coaches.

• Volvo's take over of Renault's truck business gets European Commission approval, but as one of the conditions attached to its approval the EC requires that Renault pulls out of Irisbus within two years. Irisbus was set up in January 1999 to unite the bus-building activities of Renault and Iveco.

Travel West Midland introduces a new Airbus service linking Birmingham city centre with the National Exhibition Centre and the airport. It is operated by four specially-liveried Volvo B7TLs.

London United absorbs its Stanwell Buses subsidiary.

October

Anglo American Coach Industries, importers of the Ayats coach range to the UK, abandons plans announced in October 1999 to import from Malaysia a 12m citybus, the aiRide, and two new coaches - the 3.5m-high Montana and 3.7m-high Colorado. The coaches were to have been built on MAN 18.310 underframes, and five were said to have been ordered by UK fleets. A few were sold, but not for PSV use.

A face-lifted Jonckheere Mistral body is unveiled at ExpoCoach 2000.

Long-established Abbott's of Blackpool goes in to voluntary liquidation. The company was an AEC user for many years and was still operating a few Reliances. It ran 20 coaches.

The 1,000th Bova for a UK operator is ordered by Johnsons of Henley-in-Arden.

The 10,000th Volvo B10M for an operator in the British Isles is delivered to MacPhail's of Newarthill.

Lothian Buses closes its Shrubhill Works, dating to before Edinburgh Corporation's tramway days.

Warwickshire County Council launches County Links, services operated by Guide Friday and Johnsons of Henley-in-Arden - using four Mercedes-Benz Citaros owned by the county. The Citaros are the first low-floor buses in Britain to feature three-plus-two seating. They are 48-seaters.

• The closure of Guernseybus is announced. The States of Guernsey traffic committee buys the company's vehicles and contracts the operation to Island Coachways.

• Centrebus introduces a service in Leicester between the city centre and Rushey Mead in competition with First Leicester.

November

• Arriva the Shires & Essex is named Bus Operator of the Year.

• Ensign Bus buys back London Pride, the sightseeing tour operation which it had sold in 1998. It runs 80 buses and is to be rebranded City Sightseeing, a name used for Ensign-associated operations in a number of cities around the world.

December

• The Wycombe Bus Company, part of the Go-Ahead group, is bought by Arriva the Shires. Owned by Go-Ahead since 1994, the company runs 52 vehicles.

• The London Borough of Waltham Forest buys an Optare Solo which is operated on its behalf by First Capital on a service between Chingford and the Lea Valley Leisure Centre at Picketts Lock. It's called the Pickets Lock Flier.

• Scania announce new K114 chassis to meet Euro 3 emissions legislation, which come into effect in October 2001.

• Wright announce new double-deck body, the Eclipse Gemini, for the Volvo B7TL. Arriva places an order for 50 for London.

• Bournemouth Transport buys Whippet Coaches (nine vehicles).

• The government indicates funding will be available for three guided busways - at Gatwick, Leigh and Chester. The Leigh and Chester schemes will be built on the alignment of abandoned railway lines.

• First Manchester takes over the bus operations of Coachmasters of Rochdale (19 vehicles), which had started in September 1999.

• Dublin Bus withdraws its last Bombardier double-decker. Few tears are shed.

The Coachmasters bus operations, built around school contracts, were purchased by First Manchester in December. The fleet included this former Hull Dennis Dominator with East Lancs body, seen in Wigan in the summer.

Continued growth at Arriva

ARRIVA EXPANDED significantly in 2000, with the acquisition in February of MTL Services for £34.7million. MTL was the major bus operator in Merseyside and also had two rail franchises - Merseyrail Electrics and Northern Spirit. The bus operation was renamed Arriva Merseyside.

The MTL bus fleet numbered 970 vehicles with the key trading names being MTL North, Wirral Peninsula, Southport & District and Heysham Travel. To allow the deal to proceed, the Monopolies & Mergers Commission decided that Arriva should divest itself of 30 per cent of the MTL business in Liverpool - identified as the depot at Gilmoss, which ran 120 buses. In October it was announced that Go-Ahead was the preferred bidder for Gilmoss, but the sale was not completed by the end of the year.

Having become the major operator in Merseyside, Arriva introduced some rationalisation of services which reduced its fleet in the region by around 120 buses. Another piece of rationalisation was the sale of Heysham Travel to Stagecoach in June. Heysham Travel ran 30 vehicles in and around Lancaster - 50 miles from MTL's core business in Liverpool.

Arriva quickly embarked on a massive fleet renewal to get rid of MTL's ageing Atlanteans and Titans - none of which, incidentally, was repainted in the group's corporate colours. The average age of the MTL fleet was 12 years. By the end of 2000 Arriva had introduced over 100 new buses to Merseyside and this, coupled with the fleet reduction and the withdrawal of old buses, had reduced the average age to six years.

After the MTL takeover, Arriva's other changes in 2000 were small by comparison. In February it was instructed by the Monopolies & Mergers Commission to sell Lutonian, an operation it had acquired in March 1998. It was given three months to do so, although it took until September for the company to be sold to a consortium which included Julian Peddle of the Status Group. Lutonian operated 20 minibuses.

Other changes involving Arriva the Shires saw it take over part of the operations of Town & Country in Essex in September (along with four Dennis Darts), followed in December by The Wycombe Bus Company, the Go-Ahead Group's

52-vehicle operation in High Wycombe.

This had had a convoluted history. Prior to 1990 it was part of Q-Drive's Berks Bucks Bus Co - better known as The Bee Line - and in November of that year it was sold to City of Oxford Motor Services. It became part of Go-Ahead when the Gateshead-based group bought City of Oxford in March 1994. Go further back in history and it was part of the National Bus Company's Alder Valley business, and before that was a Thames Valley operation.

The sale to Arriva, for £5million, was prompted by the impending redevelopment of the company's town centre depot and bus station, as well as by low profit margins.

Elsewhere, Arriva Cymru took over the bus operations of D&G of Rachub, near Bangor, in June, while in July there was some reorganisation in the north Midlands. This saw Arriva Midlands North take over the 55-strong Winsford operations of

Arriva's first new low-floor double-deckers for operation outside London were delivered in 2000. These included 20 Volvo B7TLs for Yorkshire. Other provincial Arriva fleets received Dennis Tridents. *David Barrow*

Arriva North West, while at the same time its four-bus Abermule outstation was transferred to Arriva Cymru.

The group's European interests expanded in November when it bought four Portuguese operators - Ami Transportes, Joao Carlos Soares & Pilhos, Abilio da Costa Moreira and Viaco Costa Lino. They run over 200 buses between them from bases in Braga, Famalicao and Guimares.

There was good news and bad news for Arriva as the year was drawing to a close. The good news was that Arriva the Shires & Essex was named bus operator of the year, in the annual bus industry awards competition. The Shires & Essex was a joint trading name adopted in February by Arriva the Shires and Arriva East Herts and Essex.

The bad news was that in an alleged dawn raid officials of the Office of Fair Trading swooped on premises of Arriva and FirstGroup as part of an enquiry into bus operations in Leeds. That was in October; by the end of the year there was no report on the nature of the OFT's investigations.

New buses for Arriva in 2000 included examples of all three of the UK's midibuses. There were over 200 Dennis Dart SLFs with Alexander ALX200 and Plaxton Pointer bodies, around 50 DAF SB120s with Wright Cadet coachwork, and 20 Volvo B6BLEs, also bodied by Wright. The SB120s were for operation in Merseyside and the north-east of England; the B6BLEs all went to Merseyside. Full-sized single-deckers were Volvo B10BLEs with Alexander and Wright bodies, and a few DAF SB220s with Alexander ALX300 bodies which went to the group's Manchester fleet.

Double-deckers were few in number, with around three dozen Alexander-bodied Dennis Tridents going to Arriva Southend, Arriva the Shires and Arriva North East, and the group's first Volvo B7TLs, 20 with ALX400 bodies, going to Arriva Yorkshire. This was the first year that new low-floor double-deckers were purchased for operations outside London. At the end of the year further B7TLs were

ARRIVA PASSENGER SERVICES

Arriva Cheshire East
Arriva Colchester
Arriva Crawley & East Surrey
Arriva Croydon & North Surrey
Arriva Cymru
Arriva Derby
Arriva Durham County
Arriva East Herts & Essex
Arriva the Shires & Essex
Arriva Fox County
Arriva Guildford & West Surrey
Arriva Kent & Sussex
Arriva Kent Thameside
Arriva Liverpool
Arriva London North
Arriva London North East
Arriva London South
Arriva Manchester
Arriva Merseyside
Arriva Midlands North
Arriva North East
Arriva North West
Arriva Northumbria
Arriva Scotland West
Arriva the Shires
Arriva the Shires & Essex

Arriva Southend
Arriva Southern Counties
Arriva Surrey & West Sussex
Arriva Tees & District
Arriva Teesside
Arriva West Sussex
Arriva Yorkshire
Arriva Yorkshire North
Arriva Yorkshire South
Arriva Yorkshire West
Leaside Travel
New Enterprise Coaches
The Original London Sightseeing Tour

Overseas operations
Arriva Danmark
Arriva Nederland
Arriva Noroeste Espana
Arriva Portugal
Arriva Sverige

Rail operations
Merseyrail Electrics
Northern Spirit

Arriva purchased MTL in February and acquired a fleet with a large number of elderly Leyland Atlanteans and Titans. These received Arriva fleetnames - but not the group's corporate colours. The Atlanteans had Alexander bodies and many were withdrawn during the year with the remainder scheduled to go in 2001.

joining the Yorkshire fleet, with Plaxton President bodies.

In London Arriva added around 100 Alexander-bodied DAF DB250 double-deckers, and small numbers of Dennis Dart SLFs with Alexander and Plaxton bodies. The big London surprise was an order for 2001 which will see Arriva getting the first double-deckers - Volvo B7TLs - to be bodied by Wright.

Interesting buses for operation in the Netherlands were 50 Darts with Alexander ALX200 bodies - marking the first big Dart order from Europe.

Replacements for MTL's old double-deckers were new single-deckers and these included relatively rare DAF SB120s with Wright Cadet bodies. Thirty were delivered in the winter of 2000-2001.

The majority of the full-size single-deckers bought by Arriva in 2000 were Volvo B10BLEs. This one, with Alexander ALX300 body, is running for Arriva the Shires and Essex.

Most of the new buses for Arriva's London operations were DAF double-deckers, but there were a few single-deckers. These were Dennis Dart SLFs with bodies by Alexander and, as seen here, Plaxton.

Volvo launches B10M replacement

WITH 10,000 SALES in the UK and Ireland in 20 years, the Volvo B10M is Britain's most successful coach chassis ever - well ahead of such legends as the Leyland Leopard or, before that, the original vertical-engined Tiger. It built on the success of Volvo's first UK model, the B58 which reached these shores in 1972. Now the B10M's reign is coming to an end, and the introduction in October 2001 of tighter new emissions regulations - Euro 3 - look as though they will bring an end to production of the 9.6-litre engine which powered the B10M.

But what hasn't come to an end is Volvo's support for the mid-engined chassis layout, something it has long championed as providing better handling and stability than rear-engined designs. In this Volvo stands alone, and to produce a mid-engined Euro 3 chassis has spent a considerable amount of money in adapting its vertical D12 truck engine to horizontal layout for the new B12M.

British coach operators are unique in Europe in preferring mid-mounted engines. Just about everywhere else rear-engined coaches are the norm. Among the advantages claimed for rear-mounted engines are easier access, high levels of parts commonality with truck engines, reduced interior noise, and massive amounts of space in the wheelbase for luggage.

Volvo is clearly hoping that the B12M will repeat the B10M's success, as B10M sales continue into 2001 and then stop when Euro 3 comes into effect. And Volvo must also be hoping that in the UK the B12M will win back sales from Iveco, MAN and Mercedes, who have been expanding steadily in the coach market, as well as from longer-established players Bova, DAF, Dennis, Neoplan, Scania and Setra.

So what does the new B12M offer? For starters, it has a stainless-steel chassis frame, using 3CR12, a material pioneered in the UK by Duple with the 425 Integral back in 1985. The frame bears no resemblance to previous Volvo models, using box sections which are laid out as a space frame to maximise the unobstructed luggage space behind the front wheels. Volvo claims the new chassis frame design saves around 200kg.

The engine will be new to most operators, although those running the few rear-engined B12Ts to be found in Britain will have some idea of its general performance. For the UK market Volvo has decided to offer only a 340bhp-rated B12M, but elsewhere there will be the option of 300, 380 and 420bhp ratings. The B10M is available with 285 and 360 bhp ratings, and Volvo is presumably expecting operators who want a lower-powered coach to buy its rear-engined 7-litre 260bhp B7R.

There are two manual gearboxes on offer, the ZF six-speed 6S-1600 and the eight-speed Volvo EGS-V, which has been developed from the previous G8 EGS. With these comes a Volvo Engine Brake as standard, but if you want more retardation a Voith 120 retarder can be fitted to ZF-equipped models, or a Volvo retarder can be built in to the EGS-V. A ZF 5HP602 five-speed automatic is also available.

The initial B12M chassis features a beam axle at the front and has drum brakes, but expect to see independent front suspension and front disc brakes in the near future.

So far B12Ms have been bodied by Berkhof, Jonckheere and Plaxton, and examples of these were on show at ExpoCoach 2000, where the new model had its UK launch in October. There were Plaxton-bodied coaches for Wallace Arnold and Flights, a Jonckheere-bodied vehicle for Dunn-Line and a Berkhof Axial 50 for Hams Coaches. Coming soon will be bodies from Caetano and Van Hool. Delivery of production chassis to coachbuilders is to start in February 2001, but most of the big Volvo coach orders announced for 2001 are for B10Ms - so don't expect to see too many B12Ms in operation until 2002.

Over the years the B10M has been the model by which other coaches have been judged.

The B12M takes the mid-engined concept forward, but makes Volvo unique in offering a coach of this layout - assuming that the onset of Euro 3 in October 2001 will see the Dennis Javelin being phased out in favour of the rear-engined R-series.

Since rear-engined coaches first became popular in the UK two decades ago there have been pundits prophesying the early demise of the mid-engined layout. Volvo clearly thinks otherwise.

The B12M will, Volvo hopes, prove to be as succesful as the B10M which it replaces in 2001. One of the first UK examples was for Dunn-Line and had Jonckheere's face-lifted Mistral bodywork which features a revised front panel with a new lighting arrangement.

London's year of the 'decker

NEW DOUBLE-DECKERS flooded the streets of London in 2001. All were low-floor models and instead of replacing the oldest buses on London's streets - Routemasters, in case anybody had forgotten - they instead replaced a variety of more recent types from time-expired Metrobuses and Titans, to Optare Spectras and four-year-old Olympians.

There are three models of low-floor double-deck chassis available in Britain, and all three were delivered to London fleets in 2000, including the capital's first Volvo B7TLs. Among the big groups, Arriva standardised on DAFs and FirstGroup and Stagecoach on Dennises. The Dennises for Stagecoach had slightly higher Alexander ALX400 bodies than on earlier deliveries, giving more interior headroom. Go-Ahead took over 200 Volvos, but also had 13 Dennises. London United took Volvos, as did Metroline although with some Dennises too. All of the bodywork was supplied by the two big players - Alexander and Plaxton - but East Lancs provided bodywork on a Volvo demonstrator for FirstGroup.

In December 1999 Harris Bus had called in the receivers who proved unable to find a buyer for the business from among existing operating groups. So London Transport stepped in and resurrected London Buses Ltd which obtained an operator's licence and took over the London tendered services which had been operated by Harris Bus. Ash Grove garage in Hackney was re-opened, and in April the operation began trading as East Thames Buses with a fleet of almost 60 vehicles which it started to repaint in traditional London red.

The idea of London Transport running its own buses was not one which filled existing operators with enthusiasm, although during 2000 the East Thames Buses business showed no signs of planning any expansion.

Another interesting new operation started in February, when Connex Bus took over operation of route 3 from London Central. Connex is, of course, a London area train operator - and not the most popular one at that. Indeed later in the year it was announced that it was to lose one of its franchises. Be that as it may, Connex Bus introduced a fleet of new Alexander-bodied Tridents to the 3, and London Central's redundant Optare Spectras were moved to Go-Ahead's operations in the north-east of England. In April Connex Bus took over a second route, the 322 from Arriva London South, and for this it used Alexander-bodied Darts.

Route 60 in south London, the subject of a debacle involving Capital Logistics and Omnibus London in the winter of 1998-99, reverted to its original operator in March, when Arriva London South took over the route and the DAFs operating it. This followed the takeover of Capital Logistics by Tellings Golden Miller.

Of course the big news in south London was the delayed opening of Croydon Tramlink, operated by FirstGroup. It started operations in May. Feeder services are operated by Orpington Buses (part of First CentreWest) using Marshall-bodied Dennis Darts in an attractive red and white livery to match that on the Bombardier articulated trams.

Much publicity, little of it positive, surrounded the Millennium Dome at Greenwich. London Central had the contract to operate two Millennium Transit services linking the Dome with Charlton Station (M1) and Greenwich Station (M2), using new DAF SB220s with East Lancs Myllennium bodies. Three of the DAFs were powered by liquefied petroleum gas. A key feature of the routes was a short stretch of high-tech guided busway using drive-by-wire technology. But that suffered from the Curse of the Dome - it didn't work. The bus lane was never used.

Metroline changed hands in February, when it was announced that the company had been bought by DelGro for £74million. The DelGro name may be unfamiliar, but most transport enthusiasts will be familiar with Singapore Bus Services, which is a DelGro subsidiary. The change of ownership brought no immediate changes in the Metroline operations. In the autumn an SBS Olympian was brought over to London to assess its suitability for use on contracts which did not require fully-accessible buses.

London Regional Transport itself underwent change, becoming Transport *for* London in April - the

Tellings Golden Miller introduced new vehicles to the 726 in the shape of seven Volvo B10BLEs with coach-seated Alexander ALX300 bodies. Alexander single-deck bodies are relatively rare on London area services.

Against the backdrop of the controversial Millennium Dome, a former Harris Bus Optare Excel freshly repainted in East Thames Buses colours.

italicised for being their choice of presentation. This is officially abbreviated to T*f*L and with that pretentious italicised f one is tempted to rhyme T*f*L with piffle.

One of TfL's first highly-visible acts in the bus world was not to support investment in low-floor, low-emission buses, but to endorse the Routemaster by actually going out and buying around 30 - from Reading Mainline, dealers and preservationists. It expected to spend around £45,000 per bus - including the purchase price and the cost of new engines - in preparing the Routemasters for service. That's about one-third of the cost of a brand-new double-decker.

The various problems associated with the Millennium Dome extended to the special services introduced to carry the millions of visitors who did not turn up in quite the numbers expected. The link services were to operate over an electronic guided busway - but thanks to technical problems it was never used. The buses were attractive DAF SB220s with East Lancs bodies and included three powered by LPG with prominent gas tanks on the roof.

MAJOR TENDER AWARDS IN 2000		
Route		**Operator**
3	Crystal Palace - Oxford Circus	London Central to Connex Bus
27	Turnham Green - Camden Town	London United to CentreWest
60	Streatham - Old Coulsdon	Capital Logistics to Arriva
70	Acton- South Kensington	CentreWest to Thorpe
200	Mitcham - Raynes Park	London Geneo Mitcham Belle
201	Mitcham - Tulse Hill	London Geneo Mitcham Belle
222	Hounslow - Uxbridge	CentreWest to London United
295	Ladbroke Grove - Clapham Jct	London Gen to CentreWest
322	Crystal Palace - Elephant & Castle	Arriva to Connex Bus
H50	West Drayton - Hayes	new route to Wings
R68	Kew Gardens -Hampton Court	London United to TGM
R70	Richmond - Hanworth	London United to TGM

New buses for London Central included Volvo B7TLs with Alexander ALX400 bodies. One loads at the Elephant & Castle.

Now, let's put this in context. Imagine First Bristol buying old Lodekkas for mainstream service. Or Stagecoach Western Buses scouring the countryside for Albion Lowlanders to refurbish. Or Arriva Midlands North deciding that BMMO D9s were the buses their customers really wanted. London's fixation with the Routemaster can at times be hard to understand. Of course it's a classic, but so's the Leyland Titan TD1 and nobody would suggest running TD1s in daily service.

Significant contracts which experienced a change of operators in 2000 included the 200 and 201 in the Mitcham area, lost by London General to Mitcham Belle. These required 22 buses and Mitcham Belle bought more Dennis Darts to cover them.

Tramlink feeder services are operated by Orpington Buses using Marshall-bodied Dennis Darts in a livery matching the trams. *Gavin Booth*

Tramlink services started in Croydon in May. The articulated trams were built by Bomabadier. *Gavin Booth*

London General also lost the 295, to CentreWest. CentreWest gained the 27 from London United in November, and was to introduce new double-deckers to the service in 2001. However to balance this gain, the 222 went from CentreWest to London United. CentreWest also lost the 70 to Thorpe and for this Thorpe added 14 new Plaxton-bodied Darts to its fleet, but in a rather simpler livery than its previous Darts, with less yellow and more red.

London United also lost two routes to Tellings Golden Miller in the summer, te R68 and R70.

A new trainlink service, the H50, was introduced in the spring, running from West Drayton to Hayes via Stockley Park, and operated by Wings using East Lancs-bodied Dennis Darts in a striking two-tone green colour scheme.

An award was announced in the autumn for a newcomer to London bus operation - Durham Travel Services. This company is to take on the 185 from Selkent in 2002 and will trade as London Easylink with a fleet of new Volvo B7TLs. Early 2001 will also see Hackney Community Transport move into big bus operation when it takes over the 153 from First Capital. It ordered Caetano-bodied Darts for the route.

Connex Bus will expand in 2001, at the expense of Arriva and London General. It won one route from each, in a round of tender awards announced in October.

TENDER AWARDS ANNOUNCED IN 2000

Route		Operator
67	Wood Green - Aldgate	First Capital to Stagecoach
118	Brixton - Morden	Arriva to London General
153	Smithfield - Finsbury Park	First Capital to Hackney
181	Lewisham - Downham	Metrobus to Selkent
185	Victoria - Lewisham	Selkent to Durham Travel
188	Russell Square - N Greenwich	Arriva to London Central
196	Norwood Junction - Brixton	London General to Connex Bus
225	Lewisham - Bermondsey	Selkent to London Central
284	Lewisham - Grove Park	Metrobus to Selkent
315	Balham Station - W Norwood	Arriva to Connex Bus
367	Croydon - Bromley	Arriva to Metrobus
368	Barking - Chadwell Heath	East London to Blue Triangle
C4	Putney Pier - Hurlingham	Thorpe to London General
C10	Victoria - Elephant & Castle	Limebourne to London Central
P3	London Bridge - New Cross Gate	Selkent to London Central
W4	Ferry Lane Est - Oakthorpe Pk	Metroline to Arriva

Bodybuilders active in the UK

Products listed for 2000 or announced in 2000 with availability in 2001.

Make & model	Body type/ length	Body height (coaches)	Chassis availability
ALEXANDER (UK)			
ALX100	minibus		Mercedes Vario
ALX200	8.8-11.3m sd		Dennis Dart SLF
			Volvo B6BLE
ALX300	12m sd		DAF SB220
			MAN 18.220NL
			Volvo B10BLE
ALX400	dd		DAF DB250
			Dennis Trident
			Volvo B7TL
ALX500	dd		Dennis Trident 3-axle
Royale	dd		Volvo Olympian
ANGLO AMERICAN (Malaysia)			
Montana	12m coach	3.5m	MAN 18.310
Colorado	12m coach	3.7m	MAN 18.400
BERKHOF (Holland)			
Radial	12m coach	3.3m	Dennis Javelin
			Volvo B10M
Axial 30	10m coach	3.3m	MAN 13.220
Axial 50	12m coach	3.55m	Dennis Javelin
			Dennis R-series
			Scania K124
			Volvo B10M
Axial 70	12m coach	3.7m	Volvo B10M
Axial 100DD	12m dd coach	4m	Scania K124
			Volvo B12T
BEULAS (Spain)			
Stergo E	12m coach	3.6m	Iveco EuroRider
El Mundo	12m coach	3.78m	Iveco EuroRider
CAETANO (UK/Portugal)			
Compass	midibus		Dennis Dart SLF
Nimbus	midibus		Dennis Dart SLF
Cutlass	12m coach	3.3m	Dennis Javelin
Enigma	8.5m coach	3.2m	MAN 11.220
Enigma	12m coach	3.5m	Dennis Javelin
			MAN 18.310
			Volvo B10M
EAST LANCS (UK)			
Spryte	midibus		Dennis Dart SLF
			Volvo B6BLE
Flyte	12m sd		MAN NL222F
			Scania L94UB
			Volvo B10M
Myllennium	12m sd		DAF SB220
Cityzen	dd		Scania N113
Lolyne	dd		Dennis Trident
Vyking	dd		Volvo B7TL
HISPANO (Spain)			
Vita	12m coach	3.5m	Mercedes O404
INDCAR (Spain)			
Maxim	midicoach		Iveco EuroMidi 80
Eco-4	midicoach		Iveco EuroMidi 95
IKARUS (Hungary)			
350	12m coach	3.3m	DAF SB3000
396	12m coach	3.55m	DAF SB3000
489	12m sd		DAF SB220
IRIZAR (Spain)			
Intercentury	12m coach	3.2m	Scania L94IB
Century	12m coach	3.5m	Scania L94IB, K124IB
Century	12m coach	3.7m	Scania K124IB 3-axle
JONCKHEERE (Belgium)			
Mistral	12m coach	3.5m	Volvo B7R, B10M, B12M
MARCOPOLO (Portugal)			
Continental 330	9.8m coach	3.3m	MAN 13.220
Continental 340	12m coach	3.45m	MAN 18.310, 18.350
			Dennis Javelin GX
Continental 360	12m coach	3.6m	MAN 24.400

Make & model	Body type/ length	Body height (coaches)	Chassis availability
MARSHALL (UK)			
Capital	midibus		Dennis Dart SLF
NEOPLAN (Germany)			
Transliner SHD	12m coach	3.5m	Dennis Javelin GX
			MAN 18.350
NOGE (Spain)			
Catalan 350	12m coach	3.5m	MAN 18.310
Catalan 370	12m coach	3.7m	MAN 24.400 3-axle
OPTARE (UK)			
Spectra	dd		DAF DB250
Nouvelle 2	minicoach		Mercedes Vario
Solera	midicoach		Mercedes O1120L
OVI (Spain)			
Versatile	12m coach	3.5m	DAF SB3000
PLAXTON (UK)			
Beaver 2	minibus		Mercedes Vario
Cheetah	minicoach		Mercedes Vario
Pointer 2	8.8-10.3m sd		Dennis Dart SLF
Prima	12m coach	3.2m	DAF SB3000
			Dennis Javelin
			Volvo B7R
Premiere 320	12m coach	3.2m	DAF SB3000
			Dennis Javelin
			Volvo B9M, B10M
Premiere 350	12m coach	3.5m	DAF SB3000
			Dennis Javelin
			Volvo B10M
Excalibur	12m coach	3.5m	Dennis Javelin
			Volvo B10M, B12T
Paragon	12m coach	3.5m	Dennis R
			Iveco EuroRider
			Volvo B10M, B12M
Panther	12m coach	3.5m	Dennis R
			Iveco EuroRider
			Volvo B10M, B12M
President	dd		DAF DB250
			Dennis Trident
			Volvo B7TL
SITCAR (Italy)			
Beluga	minicoach		Mercedes O815
SMIT (Holland)			
Stratos	10.6m coach	3.55m	DAF SB2750
VAN HOOL (Belgium)			
Alizee	12m coach	3.47m	DAF SB3000
			Scania L94, K124
			Volvo B10M
Astrobel	12m dd coach	4m	Volvo B12T
WRIGHT (UK)			
Cadet	midibus		DAF SB120
Crusader 2	midibus		Dennis Dart,
			Volvo B6BLE
Renown	12m sd		Volvo B10BLE
Axcess Floline	12m sd		Scania L94UB
Fusion	18m artic		Volvo B10LA
Solar	12m sd		Scania L94UB
Eclipse	12m sd		Volvo B7L
Eclipse Fusion	18m artic		Volvo B7TL

Coaching contrasts

Few Plaxton bodies have been built on Volvo B12 chassis. Nottingham City Coaches took two of these impressive tri-axle coaches in the spring of 2000. The Nottingham B12s have rear-mounted 380bhp Volvo D12A vertical engines and Allison automatic gearboxes.

Plaxton's new Panther and Paragon models entered service in quantity in 2000. Shearings took 10 Panthers - the first - on Volvo B10M chassis. They were air-conditioned 50-seaters, an unusually low capacity for a 12m coach.

Layston Coaches bought its first new coach in 2000 - a Dennis Javelin with Caetano Enigma bodywork. The Hertfordshire company runs just this one vehicle.

New in the Midlands

New Renowns for Oxford might conjure up images of AEC double-deckers - but in 2000 Oxford's Renowns were of the Wright variety, on Volvo B10BLE chassis. Dual-door buses are relatively uncommon outside London.

Trent has long been an Optare user and its 2000 purchases included both Solos and Excels. The round headlights show this to be the latest Excel 2.

Nottingham City Transport added new vehicles to its Pathfinder fleet in the form of long-wheelbase Optare Solos. And the wheelbase is long - at 6.23m it is comparable with that on a 12m-long B10M.

Dunn-Line introduced new buses to its park-and-ride contract in Nottingham. These were Scania L94s with Wright bodies, and they replaced East Lancs-bodied Dennis Dart SLFs.

Nottingham City Transport is one of the biggest users of Dennis Tridents outside London, with around 50 in the fleet at the end of 2000. All have East Lancs Lolyne bodies.

The 11.3m-long Super Pointer Dart found relatively few buyers when compared with the shorter variants. Whittle of Kidderminster bought two - both 38-seaters with room for a maximum of 27 standees. Compared with other Dart models, the Super Pointer Dart has a more powerful engine with a 160bhp rating, and a higher-rated Allison gearbox, the B300R instead of the standard AT545.

All change at Stagecoach

IT'S THE LIVERY enthusiasts love to hate: the ubiquitous white-with-stripes. And towards the end of the year Stagecoach announced that it's to change, as part of a major shake-up of its UK bus division. First, in September, Stagecoach announced significant changes to its British bus operations with the number of operating divisions being reduced from 19 to 12. These are shown in the accompanying table. However there was no outward sign of their existence by the end of the year and the new structure may not lead to a renaming of the operating companies - just a change of trading names.

Most of the new divisions were a logical continuation of what went before, but the Hull operations, which had been part of Cleveland Transit, were put into Stagecoach East Midlands rather than Stagecoach North East. Earlier in the year, in July, East Midlands has the number of vehicles authorised on its operating licence reduced from 206 to 180 following concerns about the company's maintenance.

Having announced a new structure for its UK bus operations, Stagecoach followed this in November with the launch of a new image. No longer will the group's British buses be white. The new base colour is grey, and the red, orange and blue stripes have metamorphosed into swoops of colour. In London, where buses have to be predominantly red, there will be upswept bands of blue and orange on the sides towards the rear. The livery was designed by Ray Stenning of Best Impressions - the man also responsible for Arriva's corporate scheme.

With the new livery come new fleetnames and a new logo, developed by an Edinburgh-based consultancy. The new look will be applied to existing vehicles as they are due for repaint. It was launched on three Alexander-bodied buses: an ALX300-bodied MAN for Fife, and two ALX400-bodied Tridents for Manchester and London. Among the first buses to be delivered in the new colours were seven Dennis Tridents with Plaxton President bodies for Cambus.

Stagecoach is also upgrading the interiors of its buses, which have in the past been serviceable rather than stylish. Key to the upgrade is the adoption of individual Lazzerini seats, and these could be found in the autumn on Tridents entering service in London and on provincial MANs - all in the old livery.

Other changes in the group's bus business in 2000 were fairly small-scale, with a number of minor acquisitions around Britain. There were two in Scotland in the spring, when Fife bought Alisons of Dunfermline, operating 30 vehicles, in April, and Bluebird followed this in May with JW Coaches of Banchory, a 13-vehicle business. The Alisons fleet was an elderly one. The most modern bus was 10 years old and the fleet's

average age was an incredible 17 years. The group's southernmost Scottish operations, Western Buses in Annan, were transferred to Cumberland Motor Services in November, along with eight buses which included six vintage Leyland Leopards with Alexander Y-type bodies.

This was Cumberland's second expansion. In June it took over Heysham Travel, which operated 30 buses in the Lancaster area. Heysham Travel was bought from Arriva. It had previously been part of the MTL group - since 1993 - and was remote from the rest of the MTL bus business on Merseyside.

Elsewhere in the north-west of England, Stagecoach Manchester fell foul of the traffic commissioner for alleged unfair competition with Dennis's. The commissioner imposed a ban on some Stagecoach routes - which was lifted when Stagecoach agreed to cease its competitive tactics, which allegedly included blocking the terminus in central Manchester with buses. Earlier in the year Stagecoach Manchester was also the subject of a complaint from UK North about unfair competition after the independent introduced a service from Manchester to Hazel Grove in May. However here the outcome was that UK North pulled off the route in July.

Stagecoach unveiled a new livery in November, and among the first buses to be delivered in it were seven Dennis Tridents with lowheight Plaxton President bodies. These were for Cambus and were the group's first Presidents. They were also the first Presidents built to a height of 4.2m (instead of 4.4m) and were 10.5m-long 78-seaters.

Stagecoach Manchester replaced some of the services which had been operated by Universal Buses of Chadderton when that company closed in April.

There were changes at Stagecoach West. In February it was announced that the green and cream livery used by Circle Line of Gloucester was to disappear and that the operation was being merged with Stagecoach Cheltenham and Gloucester. At the same time Cheltenham & Gloucester took over the Ross-on-Wye operations of Red & White, trading as Stagecoach Forest of Dean. And in September Stagecoach bought the bus operations of Phil Anslow of Pontypool, with 28 vehicles. These were absorbed by Red & White. Phil Anslow continues as a coach operator.

And reorganisation in the south at the start of the year saw Hampshire Bus acquire almost 150 vehicles from Stagecoach (South), leaving the latter operating out of Aldershot where it trades as Stagecoach Hants & Surrey.

The standard Stagecoach single-decker in fleets outside London is the MAN 18.220 with Alexander ALX300 body. This one is operated by Stagecoach Fife.

NEW LOOK FOR STAGECOACH

The new divisions announced in September 2000 were:

New division	Incorporating
Stagecoach East Scotland	Bluebird and Fife
Stagecoach West Scotland	Western
Stagecoach North East	Busways and Transit
Stagecoach North West	Ribble and Cumberland
Stagecoach Manchester	Manchester
Stagecoach East Midlands	East Midlands, Grimsby-Cleethorpes and Hull
Stagecoach South Midlands	Midland Red and Oxford
Stagecoach East	United Counties and Cambus
Stagecoach London	East London and Selkent
Stagecoach South East	Stagecoach South and East Kent
Stagecoach West and Wales	Red & White and Cheltenham & Gloucester
Stagecoach South West	Devon

New vehicles for Stagecoach were Dennis Tridents and MANs with Alexander bodies. The Tridents were mainly for London, although some went to East Kent (for a park-and-ride service) and to Manchester. The MANs were primarily for operations in Scotland and the north-west of England. There were also Dennis Darts with Plaxton bodies for a number of fleets including London. Old Plaxton-bodied Darts, with air-conditioning, joined Stagecoach's UK fleet from Hong Kong Citybus. The first entered service with Stagecoach Devon.

A hint of a possible future change in direction in vehicle purchasing came in the autumn with the appearance at the Frankfurt motor show of a Hungarian-built Ikarus E94F, based on a MAN 18.220 chassis and destined for UK trials. On the other hand it could be just a sabre-rattling exercise to keep TransBus in line. Orders for Stagecoach announced by TransBus in December comprised 184 Dennis Trident/Alexander ALX400, 102 Dennis Dart SLF/Alexander ALX200 and 50 MAN/Alexander ALX300.

In March Stagecoach bought a half share in Rapid Transit International's guided busway scheme for Northampton. And in the same month it sold Porterbrook, the railway rolling stock leasing company. It had owned the company since 1996.

Unusual additions to the Ribble fleet were two Mini Pointer Darts, allocated to the company's Clitheroe depot. Plaxton also supplied Super Pointer Darts to Cheltenham & Gloucester, Sussex Coastline and Western Buses. *Bill Potter*

STAGECOACH GROUP SUBSIDIARIES

The main Stagecoach companies and trading names in use in 2000 are listed below. These may change in 2001 with the streamlining of the group's UK bus division as shown in the table on page 33.

Bayline
   Stagecoach Devon
Bluebird Buses
   Inverness Traction
   JW Coaches
   Stagecoach
Burnley & Pendle Transport
   Stagecoach Ribble
Busways Travel Services
   Magic Bus
   Stagecoach Busways
Cambus group
   Cambus
   Viscount Bus & Coach
Cleveland Transit
   Stagecoach Darlington
   Stagecoach Hartlepool
   Stagecoach Kingston-upon-Hull
   Stagecoach Transit
Devon General
   Stagecoach Devon
East Kent Road Car
East London Bus & Coach Co
East Midland Motor Services
   Chesterfield Transport
Fife Scottish Omnibuses
Greater Manchester Buses South
   Magic Bus
   Stagecoach Manchester
Grimsby-Cleethorpes Transport Co
Hampshire Bus
Magicbus Scotland (Holding
company)
National Transport Tokens (99.9%)

Parfitt's Motor Services
PSV Claims Bureau
Rapid Transit International (50%)
Rhondda Buses
Ribble Motor Services
Scottish Highway Express
South Coast Buses
South East London & Kent Bus Co
   Stagecoach Selkent
Stagecoach Devon
Stagecoach East Kent
Stagecoach Forest of Dean
Stagecoach Glasgow
Stagecoach Graphics
Stagecoach International Services
Stagecoach North West
   Cumberland Motor Services
   Coachlines
      Lakeland Experience
      Stagecoach Lancaster
Stagecoach Scotland
Stagecoach South
   Stagecoach Hants & Surrey
Stagecoach West
   Aberdare Bus Co
   Cheltenham & Gloucester
   Omnibus Co
      Gloucester Citybus
      Metro
      Stroud Valleys
   Cheltenham District Traction
   Midland Red (South)
   Red & White Services
   Swindon & District

Sussex Coastline
Thames Transit
   The Oxford Tube
   Stagecoach Oxford
United Counties Omnibus Co
   Coachlink
The Valleys Bus Co
Western Buses
   AA Buses
   A1 Service

Overseas operations
Coach Canada
Coach USA
Eastbourne Bus Company (New
Zealand)
Hong Kong Citybus
Hong Kong Kwoon Chung
(Chongqing) (45%)
Stagecoach Australia
Stagecoach Portugal
Stagecoach Wellington (New
Zealand)
Wellington City Transport (New
Zealand)
Yellow Bus Co (New Zealand)
   Whenuapai Bus Travel

Rail operations
The Island Line
Sheffield Supertram
South West Trains
Virgin Rail (49%)

Dennis expands coach range

Dennis announced a new version of its rear-engined R-series coach underframe at ExpoCoach 2000 in October - before any of the original model, announced 12 months earlier, had entered revenue-earning service.

The original R-series, which is being bodied by Plaxton, uses a Cummins ISM 11-litre engine, with 340 and 410bhp power ratings - the latter uprated from the 405bhp announced when it was launched. The new variant, to be bodied by Berkhof, features a 300bhp 8.3-litre Cummins ISC engine.

The modular underframe and running gear of the R300 are unchanged from the R340 and R410, with independent front suspension, disc brakes and a choice of gearboxes - ZF six-speed manual or ASTronic 10-speed automated. The R-series was developed by Dennis using front and rear modules for integration into the completed coach body, a design which eliminates the conventional chassis frame to reduce weight and allow the bodybuilder to maximise luggage capacity.

However the Dennis name is being kept in the background, with the R340 and R410 being promoted as the Plaxton R-series, and the ISC-powered model as the Berkhof R300. The R300 will have Berkhof's Axial 50 body, and a small number should enter service in 2001 with the first being destined for Banstead Coaches, a company which operates Berkhof-bodied Dennis Javelins.

Officially, the new model is an addition to the Dennis range but some industry observers expect to see the Javelin being phased out in 2001 before the Euro 3 exhaust emissions limits come in to force in October.

Meanwhile, Plaxton R-series prototypes were undergoing extensive tests during the year. One was operating between London and Bath, over the same route and to the same running times as a National Express service. The route was chosen to give a range of operating conditions, from congestion around the capital to 100km/hr running on parts of the M4. Another was running back and forwards to Spain.

The first orders for Plaxton R-series coaches were announced in the autumn - 13 for Hallmark and four for Whittle of Kidderminster, all to be delivered in 2001.

As part of its proving trials Dennis operated this prototype R-series between Bath and London during the summer on a schedule which shadowed a National Express working. The travel-stained coach, with Plaxton Paragon body, pauses in Swindon bus station on an early morning run.

Optare passes to US ownership

While British operators and manufacturers are showing a strong interest in the US bus and coach industry, the interest isn't all one way and in January North American Bus Industries (NABI) acquired Optare in a £21.5million deal.

NABI is in fact the American subsidiary of a Hungarian company and the enlarged NABI operation employs some 1,400 people - including 440 at Optare - and in 2000 built around 1,000 buses.

In announcing the takeover, NABI revealed that Optare was developing a new integral double-decker with a full-length low floor, allegedly to be ready for launch by the end of 2000 but in reality still some way off.

NABI designs and part-builds buses in Hungary for completion in the USA. Its US operation also builds composite buses using a technique not unlike that used to make the hulls of yachts. NABI was created in 1992, taking over the North American Ikarus operations.

An early development following the takeover was work on a 30ft-long Solo for the US market, and in August an order was announced for 75 for American Eagle Airlines for delivery in 2001.

In the spring Optare announced the Solera 2 coach for the UK market which is longer than the original model - 9.95m against 9.2m - and is based on the Mercedes-Benz Atego 1223L chassis rather than the old O1120L. The 39-seat Solera 2 is built in Spain by Ferqui and is powered by a Mercedes OM906LA engine rated at 230bhp - a figure which not so long ago would have seemed quite respectable for a heavy-duty 12m coach.

New from Optare in 2000 was a minibus developed as CTV2000 and launched in August as the

Alero, a model which continues the Optare tradition of taking bus design to new heights. The Alero is targeted at the welfare market and is a low-floor model with room for up to 16 passengers. It brings new style and ease of access to a market sector which has long been dominated by converted vans or by small buses with bodies which look as if they've been knocked up in somebody's back yard using whatever materials came to hand.

The Alero - which resembles a big people carrier rather than a small bus - uses a one-piece composite body shell which cuts weight and eliminates corrosion. Stainless steel tubes provide an integral frame within the shell. The composite material is colour

The stylish Solo has won new customers for Optare and has helped hasten the demise of truck-based minibuses for local bus operation. HA Coaches of Shotts took a sizeable fleet, primarily for Strathclyde PTE contracts. This one is operating in Ay

impregnated and buyers have the choice of five colours - Snow White, Ardanza Red, Corn Yellow Atlanta Blue and Dolphin Green. I is 2.1m wide and 7.2m long, and with its kneeling suspension can provide an entrance step height of just 180mm, eliminating the need for a wheelchair lift. The entrance is immediately behind the front wheel. It weighs around 3.5 tonnes with a gross vehicle weight of 6 tonnes maximum.

Optare's Spectra set the double-deck style revolution going, but as other manufacturers have caught up, so Spectra sales have slowed down. Wilts & Dorset took six in 2000. The Spectra is built on the DAF DB250 chassis.

The engine is mounted at the front and is a 2.8-litre Iveco diesel rated at 125bhp - basically the same engine as used in the TurboDaily range of vans and light trucks. A six-speed ZF gearbox takes the drive to the rear axle. The Alero has independent front suspension and front disc brakes.

The continuing success of the Solo has brought an end to production of the MetroRider, of which just a few were delivered during 2000. The MetroRider has a long and - under Optare ownership at least - honourable history, although the original MCW-built vehicles were not quite so highly regarded. MCW launched its integral minibus at the 1986 Motor Show and had sold just over 1,000 by the time the company closed.

Optare took over the production rights in 1989 and set about a major revamp, addressing the shortcomings of the original MCW product. Optare rationalised the range, standardising on the 5.9-litre Cummins B-series engine and Allison AT545 gearbox. It offered two lengths, 7m and 8.4m, and on the longer model there was a choice of widths, 2.21m and 2.38m. All short MetroRiders were built to the narrower width.

A Series 3 model was introduced in 1993 with new styling, an uprated Cummins Euro 1 engine, and an added 7.7m-long version. This was followed by the Series 4 in 1996, which met Euro 2 emission limits and had a revised entrance to improve accessibility. The Series 4 was available in two lengths, 7.7m and 8.5m, and in the same two widths as before. The frontal styling was changed slightly. Optare's MetroRider production totalled around 1,100 vehicles.

New products in the pipeline in 2000 were an integral low-floor double-decker - with some reports suggesting it might have a side-mounted engine - and a 12m single-decker based on the Renault Agora Line. Agora Line underframes were delivered to Optare during the year but work on the project was put on hold when Irisbus - of which Renault is a part - faced uncertainty about its future structure and ownership.

Above: The first left-hand-drive Excel was built in 2000 and exhibited at a trade show in Hungary - a country connected to Optare's new parent company, North American Bus Industries.

Below: The Alero is Optare's new integral minibus, designed primarily for the welfare market - an area where up till now style in buses has been distinctly lacking.

New in the North West

Finglands - which is part of the EYMS Group - took delivery of four new double-deckers in 2000. Two were Plaxton-bodied Volvo B7TLs, as seen here in central Manchester; the other two were Dennis Tridents with Alexander bodies. A similar combination of four buses was delivered to East Yorkshire.
David Barrow

For its first new double-decker Dennis's Coaches of Dukinfield initially adopted a red and yellow livery - but subsequent deliveries were in the standard red and grey, to avoid confusion with the colours of First PMT. This bus, an East Lancs-bodied Trident, was repainted to match.
David Barrow

The first double-decker for JP Travel of Middleton entered service at the end of the year. It was a Volvo B7TL with East Lancs Vyking body.

Low-floor double-deckers were introduced to the Isle of Man in 2000, with the first being a batch of six Dennis Tridents with East Lancs Lolyne bodies which entered service in the summer. More followed later in the year, along with three Optare Spectras.

Bullock of Cheadle was the first operator to run low-floor double-deckers in the north-west, with two Optare Spectras in 1998. Additions to the fleet in 2000 included East Lancs-bodied Dennis Tridents. *David Barrow*

Customers for the distinctive East Lancs Myllennium body on the DAF SB220 chassis included Blue Bus of Horwich. Like most new additions to the Blue Bus fleet it carries an appropriate BLU registration. *David Barrow*

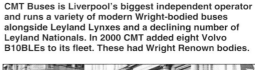

The Mini Pointer Dart found a ready market among operators large and small in 2000. Liverpool City Bus added one to its fleet. It replaced an older step-entrance bus on a Merseytravel contract serving a hospital in Liverpool.

CMT Buses is Liverpool's biggest independent operator and runs a variety of modern Wright-bodied buses alongside Leyland Lynxes and a declining number of Leyland Nationals. In 2000 CMT added eight Volvo B10BLEs to its fleet. These had Wright Renown bodies.

Who owns whom...

A quick guide to the major groups and their key subsidiary companies, associated companies and principal trading names.

Appleby
R W Appleby
Fleetjet
   North Bank Travel
Halcyon Leisure

Arriva - see page 19

Blackpool Transport Services
Handy Bus

Blazefield Holdings
Harrogate & District Travel
Huntingdon & District
Keighley & District Travel
Premier Buses
Sovereign Bus & Coach Co
Sovereign Buses (London)
   London Sovereign
Yorkshire Coastliner

Bournemouth Transport
Christchurch Buses
Dorset Travel Services
   Whippet Coaches
Vintage Yellow Buses
Yellow Buses
Yellow Coaches

CMT Buses
ABC Travel

Dunn-Line Group
Ascot Coaches
Dunn-Line Travel
Dunn-Line (Derby)
Dunn-Line (Holdings)
Dunn-Line (London)
Dunn-Line (UK)
Dunn-Line (West Midlands)
Lamcote Motors (Radcliffe)
Nottingham Coach Co
Seamarks
Stevensons

EYMS Group
East Yorkshire Motor Services
Finglands
Scarborough & District Motor Services

FirstGroup - see page 12

Flights Travel Group
Excelsior Coachways
Flights Coach Travel

Go-Ahead Group
Brighton & Hove Bus and Coach Co
City of Oxford Motor Services
   The Oxford Bus Company
   Oxford Express
Go North East
   Go Gateshead
   Go Xpress
   Go Northern
   Go Wear Buses
   Go Coastline
London Central Bus Co
London General Transport Services
Metrobus
UK rail operations
Thameslink (65%)
Victory Railways (65%)
   Thames Trains

Lothian Buses plc
Dormant companies:
Edinburgh Bus and Coach
Edinburgh Buses
Edinburgh City Bus
Edinburgh City Transport
Lothian Bus and Coach
Lothian Region Transport

Metroline Holdings
Brents Travel
Metroline London Northern
Metroline Travel
Scottish Citylink
Skye-ways (25%)
West Coast Motors (25%)
   Oban & District

Moseley Group
Bowens
Yorks

National Express Group
Airlinks The Airport Coach Company
   Airbus
   Cambridge Coach Services
   Jetlink
   Silverwing
   Speedlink
ATC Group (USA)
Kenneth E Bauman Bus (USA)
Crabtree-Harmon (USA)
Durham Transportation (USA)
Eurolines (Nederland)
Eurolines (UK)
Flightlink
GoByCoach.com
Group Bronckaers (Belgium)
National Bus Company (Australia)
   Westbus (UK)
National Express
National Expressliners
Robinsons Bus Service Inc (USA)
School Services & Leasing (USA)
Taybus Holdings
   Tayside Public Transport Co
   Travel Dundee
   Travel Greyhound
   G&M Wishart
Transport Management Group
(Australia)
West Midlands Travel Group
   Smiths Coaches (Shennington)
   Travel Merry Hill
   Travel Your Bus
   Travel West Midlands
   West Midlands Travel
UK rail operations
c2c
Cardiff Railways
Central Trains
Gatwick Express
London & Continental Railways (17%)
Midland Mainline
ScotRail
Silverlink
Travel Midland Metro
Wales and West
West Anglia Great Northern

**Northern Ireland Transport Holding
Company/Translink**
Citybus
Flexibus
Ulsterbus
   BusyBus
   Goldliner
NI Railways

Nottingham City Transport
Pathfinder
South Notts

Parks of Hamilton
Trathens Travel Services

**The Go-Ahead Group's interests
include City of Oxford Motor Services**

Yorkshire Traction is the keystone of the Traction Group. Its fleet includes East Lancs-bodied Volvo B6BLEs.

Rapson group
Highland Bus & Coach
Highland Country Buses
Peace's Coaches
Rapson's Coaches
Shalders Coaches

Reading Transport
Goldline Travel
London Line
Newbury Buses
Reading Buses

Rossendale Transport
Ellen Smith Coaches

Southern Vectis
Musterphantom
    Solent Blue Line
Southern Vectis Omnibus Co

Stagecoach - see page 34

Status Bus & Coach
Bakers Coaches, Biddulph
Burtons Coaches, Haverhill
    Premier Travel
Classic Coaches, Annfield Plane
    Primrose
Hylton Castle, South Hylton
Link Line, London
MK Metro, Milton Keynes
Midland Choice Travel
Moor Dale Coaches, South Hylton
Stratford Blue Travel
Tellings Golden Miller, London
TGM Logistics, London

Thamesdown Transport
Dormant companies:
Swindon Buses
Swindon Citybus
Swindon Coaches
Swindon Transport
Thamesdown Coaches

Traction Group
Andrews (Sheffield)
    Yorkshire Terrier
Barnsley & District Traction Co
Lincolnshire Road Car Co
Meffan (Kirriemuir)
Metropolitan Omnibus (London) (part)
    London Traveller
Strathtay Scottish
Yorkshire Traction Co
    Coachlink
    Fastlink
    Townlink

Transdev
London United Busways
Nottingham City Transport (18%)

Tellings Golden Miller, operator of this Setra S315 is part of the Status Group.

Wellglade
Barton Buses
Kinchbus
Nottinghamshire & Derbyshire
    Blue Apple
Trent Buses

Wilts & Dorset
Hants & Dorset Motor Services
    Damory Coaches
Levers Coaches
Tourist Coaches
    Bell
Wilts & Dorset Bus Co

MANUFACTURING GROUPS

EvoBus
Mercedes-Benz
Kassbohrer
    Setra

Henlys
Blue Bird (USA)
Prevost (Canada) (49%)
    NovaBus
TransBus International (30%)

Irisbus
Ikarus (57.7%)
Iveco Bus
Heuliez
Karosa

Orlandi
Renault Bus

MAN
ERF
Neoplan

Mayflower
Thomas Dennis (49%)
TransBus International (70%)

TransBus International
Alexander
Dennis
Kirkby Coach & Bus
Metsec
Plaxton Scarborough
Plaxton Wigan

VDL Group
DAF Bus
Berkhof
Jonckheere
Smit

Volvo Bus
Carrus Oy
Drogmoller
Henlys (10%)
MASA
Prevost (Canada) (51%)
    NovaBus
Steyr
Volvo Coach Sales

Wright joins the double-deck fray

THE ENTRY OF a new manufacturer to the double-deck body market is a rare event. If you discount Optare, on the basis that it was a continuation of the Charles H Roe business, the last newcomer to double-deck body production in the UK was Marshall of Cambridge, back in 1978. Marshall ceased building double-deckers in 1983.

But in 2001 an all-new double-deck design from Wrightbus of Ballymena is set to take to Britain's road. The new model will be the company's first-ever double-decker and is being built on the Volvo B7TL. It is to be called the Eclipse Gemini, a play on the zodiac sign for twins - in this case twin decks.

The Eclipse Gemini was announced in December, as the merger between Mayflower and Henlys was given the go-ahead. The union of Alexander and Plaxton will ultimately lead to a reduction in choice for double-deck buyers, and it may be that Volvo was concerned that almost 99 per cent of its double-deck chassis in the UK are being bodied by a group which now incorporates rival chassis builder Dennis.

The Eclipse Gemini is styled to resemble the latest generation of Wright single-deckers, and will use a similar method of construction. It gives Wright a comprehensive range of urban bus bodies, with a family of designs which embraces midibuses, full-size single-deckers, artics, and now a double-decker. The only gap in its bus range is a minibus - but that is a market sector which has shrunk dramatically in recent years.

The interior styling will echo that of the single-deck 12m Eclipse and the 18m articulated Eclipse Fusion, with an ergonomically-

Company	Model	DAF DB250	Dennis Trident	Volvo B7TL
BRITAIN'S DOUBLE-DECK BUILDERS				
		Chassis availability		
Alexander	ALX400	x	x	x
East Lancs	Lolyne/Vyking		x	x
Optare	Spectra	x		
Plaxton	President	x	x	x
Wrightbus	Eclipse Gemini			x

designed work station for the driver and a bright and modern travelling environment for passengers. The windscreen wipers will be located at the top of the windscreen which improves the driver's visibility and also means the wiper motors are less likely to be damaged in an accident.

Full air-conditioning will be available, and the Eclipse Gemini will have multiplex wiring, with the option of a full diagnostic system. Other noteworthy features planned for the Eclipse Gemini's electrics include the option of long-life LED rear lights to eliminate frequent bulb changes.

There are to be two variants - one 10.2m long, the other 10.7m in length. Operators will be able to specify one or two doors, and gasket or bonded tinted glazing. Typical seating capacities will be 68 for the 10.2m bus and 74 for the longer version.

The announcement of the new Wrightbus model was accompanied by an order for 50 from Arriva for service in London. Arriva has been a major customer for Wright single-deckers for its operations outside London, and has bought double-deckers from both Plaxton and Alexander. It will continue to dual source double-deckers, with Plaxton Presidents on order for 2001.

Demand for new double-deckers is in long-term decline, as a quick look at the make-up of many urban fleets will show - new double-deckers are relatively uncommon in some cities such as Glasgow, Liverpool and Sheffield, where the double-decker once reigned supreme.

With signs of imminent over-capacity amongst double-deck body manufacturers, the arrival the Eclipse Gemini is bound to create a few waves.

An artist's impression of the new Wright double-decker. Production starts in 2001.

New in the North East and Yorkshire

Interesting new double-deckers for Go-Ahead in the north-east were Dennis Tridents with East Lancs bodies. While the group operates a substantial fleet of Dennis single-deckers, these were the first double-deckers for use in this area although similar buses are in operation with Brighton & Hove. On a grey day in Gateshead the Whitley Bay Holiday Park holds out the promise of something more pleasurable... *David Barrow*

Thornes of Bubwith added this distinctive bus to its fleet - an East Lancs-bodied DAF SB220. The government's commitment to improving rural bus services saw a number of small operators investing in new buses in 2000. *David Barrow*

Keighley & District added Volvo B10BLEs with Wright Renown bodies to its fleet in 2000. Similar buses were delivered to sister Blazefield companies Sovereign Bus & Coach and Harrogate & District. *David Barrow*

The school run

It is the need to move school pupils which dictates the size of most bus operators' and many coach operators' fleets. Home-to-school transport is big business and its an area which attracts some controversy.

There are those who criticise the use of elderly coaches and double-deckers on school contracts. To this the operators' response is straightforward: if councils pursue the lowest price for contracts they can't expect modern vehicles. And there are also issues about behavioural standards on school buses - with rowdy kids vandalising interiors.

Then there's the growing concern about the congestion caused by parents running their children to school in the family car. That is perhaps contributing to the rise in obesity among children - they no longer get enough exercise.

During 2000 there were a few initiatives on the school transport issue which might bear fruit - or which again, might not.

FirstGroup imported a US Blue Bird school bus, produced by a subsidiary of the Henlys Group which owned Plaxton and is now a minority partner in TransBus International. This used familiar components - Cummins engine, Allison gearbox - but in the unfamiliar setting of a rugged yellow American-style school bus. With three-and-two seating it could, in theory, offer up to around 70 seats -

which means that it could replace an old double-decker.

The FirstGroup Blue Bird differed from the few Blue Birds currently in UK operation which are heavier-duty rear-engined models.

Used vehicle dealer Fleetmaster Bus & Coach announced it's answer to the school transport problem in the autumn. Fleetmaster can provide an East Lancs Hyline body on a refurbished Leyland Tiger chassis to provide a modern bus with up to 70 seats and with prices starting from around £64,000. The Hyline looks like the low-floor Myllennium but its higher build is designed for fitment to mid-engined chassis. Four entered service with Strathtay Scottish in the summer.

High-capacity double-deckers are another option, and FirstGroup imported three-axle Olympians from Hong Kong for use on school services in Greater Manchester. Ensignbus, the Essex dealer, was advertising ex-Hong Kong three-axle Metrobuses for sale as potential school contract vehicles in the UK, although none were sold in 2000. And Metroline, exploring its new links with Singapore, imported an ex-Singapore Bus Services Olympian to see if it would be suitable for contract work. It is expected to enter service in 2001.

Irisbus also sees potential to supply school buses to the UK, using a front-engined chassis derived from the Iveco EuroCargo. It announced in September that it would be selling

a low-cost bus - around £80,000 - with 70-seat bodywork produced by an un-named mainland European builder. Irisbus argues that the EuroCargo is familiar to many local authorities who use it in their truck fleets. The EuroCargo is sold with Ford badging in the UK - how about calling the new model the Ford R-series....

In recent years Plaxton has offered its Prima body - a low-cost Premiere 320 - with three-plus-two seating for up to 69 passengers. However it's a model which has found few takers, partly because it compromises comfort and restricts the use which can be made of the coach. Caetano has done the same with its Cutlass body on the Dennis Javelin chassis, again with but limited success.

In the end, the problem comes down to money. Home-to-school contracts operate for around 190 days a year and for a few hours each day, which offers poor utilisation of vehicles. To run relatively expensive purpose-built single-deck buses in place of old coaches or double-deckers would require a re-examination by tendering authorities of the whole financial basis of school contracts - which seems just a bit unlikely.

So for enthusiasts of older vehicles there would seem to be little to fear. The widespread appearance of high-quality vehicles on school contracts is still a long way off.

Much smarter than the average elderly school bus - but otherwise typifing the type - is this immaculate 20-year-old Atlantean seen in Blackburn running for Stagecoach Ribble. It is one of very few Atlanteans left in a fleet which had pioneered the type.

This Blue Bird was imported to the UK on behalf of FirstGroup as a possible alternative to using elderly buses on school services. *John Burnett*

Web index

The websites for major operators and manufacturers mentioned are detailed below. For the major bus operating groups the main group sites will usually provide links to individual operating subsidiaries. For international manufacturers the address given is for whichever website is most appropriate to their UK activities.

Airlinks..www.airlinks.co.uk
Alexander ....www.walexander.co.uk
Arriva ....www.arriva.co.uk
Ayats ....www.angloamericancoaches.com
Berkhof ....www.berkhof.net
Blackburn..........................www.blackburntransport.co.uk
Bluebird, Manchester ....www.bluebirdbus.co.uk
Bournemouth Tran ....www.yellowbuses.co.uk
Bova ....www.bova.nl
Brighton & Hove....................................www.buses.co.uk
Bus Eireann ....www.buseireann.ie
Caetano ....www.caetano.co.uk
Cardiff Bus ....www.cardiffbus.com
Coach USA ....www.coachusa.com
Connex Bus.......................................www.connexbus.co.uk
Dennis ....www.dennisbus.com
Dublin Bus ....www.dublinbus.ie
Dunn-Line..www.dunn-line.co.uk
East Yorkshire ....www.eyms.co.uk
Ensignbus...www.ensignbus.com
EvoBus ....www.evobus.com
Finglands ....www.finglands.co.uk
First Aberdeen............................www.firstaberdeen.co.uk
First Badgerline ....www.firstbadgerline.co.uk
First Beeline ....www.firstbeeline.co.uk
First Bradford............................www.firstbradford.co.uk
First Calderline ....www.firstcalderline.co.uk
First Capital....................................www.firstcapital.co.uk
First CentreWest.....................www.firstcentrewest.co.uk
First Cityline ....www.firstcityline.co.uk
First Cymru ....www.firstcymru.co.uk
First Eastern National ......www.firsteasternnational.co.uk
First Edinburgh ....www.firstedinburgh.co.uk
First Glasgow ....www.firstglasgow.co.uk
FirstGroup ....www.firstgroup.com
First Huddersfield ....www.firsthuddersfield.co.uk
First Leeds ....www.firstleeds.co.uk
First Leicester...........................www.firstleicester.co.uk
First Mainline ....www.firstmainline.co.uk
First Midland Red ....www.firstmidlandred.co.uk
First Northampton...............www.firstnorthampton.co.uk
First Provincial ....www.firsthampshire.co.uk
First Red Bus ....www.firstredbus.co.uk
First Southampton...............www.firstsouthampton.co.uk
First Southern National www.firstsouthernnational.co.uk
First Thamesway ....www.firstthamesway.co.uk
First Western National ....www.firstwesternnational.co.uk
First York ....www.firstyork.co.uk

Flights Coaches ....www.motorcoach.co.uk
Go-Ahead ....www.go-ahead.com
Henlys ....www.henlys.com
Hong Kong Citybus.........................www.citybus.com.hk
Irisbus ....www.irisbus.com
Jonckheere ....www.jonckheere.be
London Transport ....www.londontransport.co.uk
London's
Transport Museum ....www.ltmuseum.co.uk
Lothian Buses ....www.lothianbuses.co.uk
MAN ....www.man.co.uk
Marshall ....www.marshallsv.co.uk
Mayflower ....www.mayf.co.uk
Mayne, Manchester ....www.mayne.co.uk
Metrobus ....www.metrobus.co.uk
Metroline ....www.metroline.co.uk
Metsec ....www.duplemetsec.co.uk
National Express ....www.nationalexpressgroup.com
Neoplan ....www.neoplan.com
Nottingham City Tpt ....www.nctx.co.uk
Optare ....www.optare.com
Oxford Bus Company ....www.oxfordbus.co.uk
Plaxton ....www.plaxton.co.uk
Pete's Travel ....www.petestravel.co.uk
Rapsons ....www.rapsons.co.uk
Reading Buses ....www.reading-buses.co.uk
SC Coachbuilders ....www.caetano.co.uk
Scania..www.scania.com
Scottish Citylink ....www.citylink.co.uk
Solent Blueline ....www.solentblueline.co.uk
Southern Vectis.........................www.southernvectis.com
Stagecoach...................................www.stagecoachplc.com
Stagecoach Cambus ....www.stagecoach-cambus.co.uk
Stagecoach Hull ....www.stagecoach-hull.co.uk
Stagecoach London ....www.stagecoach-london.co.uk
Stagecoach Oxford...........www.stagecoach-oxford.co.uk
Stagecoah Transit ....www.stagecoach-transit.co.uk
Stagecoach
United Counties ....www.stagecoachuc.co.uk
Stagecoach
Western ....www.stagecoach-westernbuses.co.uk
Transbus ....www.transbusint.com
Travel West Midlands....................www.travelwm.co.uk
Trent..www.trentbuses.co.uk
Truronian...www.truronian.co.uk
Volvo ....www.volvobuses.volvo.co.uk
Warrington ....www.warringtonboroughtransport.co.uk
Wright..www.wright-bus.co.uk

The end of the Olympian

BRITAIN'S MOST SUCCESSFUL double-deck design of recent years reached the end of the road in the summer, with the delivery of the last Volvo Olympians to Yorkshire Coastliner. However while the Olympian may have ceased in the UK, an export derivative is still produced in Poland for Hong Kong - the low-entry three-axle Super Olympian.

The Olympian was launched in 1980 by Leyland as a replacement for the Atlantean, Fleetline and Bristol VRT. It offered an improved specification with air suspension (the old models had leaf springs) and a retarder. And it had a perimeter frame in place of the conventional ladder type of the previous generation of double-deck chassis.

In its original form it had the choice of Leyland TL11 or Gardner 6LXB engines, driving through a Leyland Hydracyclic gearbox. It had air suspension; the option of coil springs was investigated but not pursued.

Bodywork in the early days was available from Alexander, East Lancs, ECW, Marshall, Northern Counties and Roe. Alexander fitted the first example of its new R-type body to one of the pre-production Olympian chassis, and offered R-types (and, later, Royales) right up to the end of Olympian manufacture. ECW and Roe built bodies derived from the Leyland Titan integral, and when Roe closed similar bodies were built in small numbers by Optare. Marshall bodied only one batch of Olympians, for Bournemouth Transport.

Early customers included London Transport, the National Bus Company, the Scottish Bus Group, the passenger transport executives at Greater Manchester, Merseyside, South Yorkshire, Strathclyde and West Yorkshire, and some significant municipal fleets such as Cardiff, Grampian, Lothian and Warrington.

For bus use there was a choice of two wheelbases for a nominal overall length of 9.5 and 10m, while a longer wheelbase was produced for a small number of commuter coaches. A three-axle variant was built for export, with Hong Kong being the key market. Changes over the years included the availability of a Cummins L10 engine from 1985, and the option of Voith and ZF gearboxes. The L10 replaced Leyland's TL11 in 1988, and Leyland's Hydracyclic gearbox was phased out at the same time. The Cummins/ZF combination became the preferred choice for most fleets.

From 1983 the Olympian was Britain's best-selling double-decker, although sales plummeted when deregulation and privatisation created a climate of uncertainty in the mid-1980s. That uncertainty hit a number of manufacturers hard and, following a management buy-out in 1987, Leyland Bus was sold to Volvo in 1988.

The Olympian continued under Volvo ownership, initially with Leyland badging, but it metamorphosed into a Volvo, with Volvo's 9.6-litre engine being offered in an updated chassis which was introduced in 1993. This originally retained the option of a Cummins L10 engine (but not a Gardner) and the L10 remained

available until 1996 when it was replaced at Cummins by the M11, which Volvo opted not to engineer into the Olympian.

In post-deregulation Britain the Olympian was clear leader in double-deck sales. It was the Stagecoach group standard, with bodywork by Alexander and Northern Counties, until superseded by the Dennis Trident. It was also bought by Arriva and FirstGroup, and was the choice of most London operators from the late 1980s with significant numbers entering service in the capital.

Over a 20 year production life 10,268 Olympians were built, including 5,413 Volvo-badged buses from Irvine in the last eight years of manufacture. Considering how much the bus industry has changed over that period, it is surprising to realise that production actually peaked in the mid-1990s, with over 1,000 chassis being built by Volvo in 1996 and again in 1997. By comparison, in the early 1980s annual output by Leyland was around half that figure.

Of the 10,000-plus Olympians built, the vast majority are still in operation, including some of the first few W-registered buses - W-suffixed, that is. And it's a pleasant symmetry that the last British Olympians, the batch for Yorkshire Coastliner, should also be W-registered.

End of the line. One of the last Olympians nears completion at Alexander.

Deliveries 2000

New deliveries in 2000 included the following:

Operator	Qty	Chassis	Body
Aintree Coachline	1	Dennis Trident	East Lancs Lolyne
Airlinks, London	17	DAF SB220	East Lancs Myllennium
Alpha, Hull	5	Dennis Dart SLF	Plaxton Pointer 2
Amos, Daventry	5	Dennis Dart SLF	Caetano Nimbus
Appleby	2	Volvo B6BLE	Wright
	1	Dennis Dart SLF	Caetano
Armchair, Brentford	4	Volvo B10M	Van Hool Alizee
Arriva Derby	12	Dennis Dart SLF	Alexander ALX200
		Dennis Dart SLF	Plaxton Pointer 2
Arriva Netherlands		Dennis Dart SLF	Alexander ALX200
Arriva North East	22	DAF SB120	Wright Cadet
	8	Dennis Dart SLF	Plaxton Pointer 2
Arriva North West	50	Dennis Dart SLF	Plaxton Pointer 2
	30	DAF SB120	Wright Cadet (b)
	20	Volvo B6BLE	Wright Crusader
	9	Dennis Dart SLF	Alexander ALX200
Arriva Southend	15	Dennis Trident	Alexander ALX400
Arriva Yorkshire	28	Dennis Dart SLF	Plaxton Pointer 2
	20	Volvo B7TL	Alexander ALX400
	20	Volvo B7TL	Plaxton President (b)
	6	Volvo B10BLE	Wright Renown
Astons, Kempsey	2	Dennis Dart SLF	Plaxton Pointer 2
	1	Scania N113	East Lancs Cityzen
Bebb, Llantwit Fardre	5	Optare Solo	
BC Transit	11	Dennis Trident	Duple Metsec
Black Prince, Leeds	1	Optare MetroRider 4	
Blue Bus, Horwich	1	DAF SB220	East Lancs Myllennium
	3	Dennis Dart SLF	Plaxton Pointer 2
	1	Volvo B10BLE	Wright Renown
Bluebird, Manchester	3	Dennis Dart SLF	East Lancs Spryte
Bowers, Chapel-en-le-Frith	2	Optare Solo	
Brighton & Hove	20	Dennis Trident	East Lancs Lolyne
Bullock, Cheadle	5	Dennis Trident	East Lancs Lolyne
	4	Scania N113	East Lancs Cityzen
Bus Eireann	20	Volvo B6BLE	Wright Crusader II (a)
	20	Volvo B10BLE	Wright Renown
	20	Mercedes Citaro	
	21	Dennis Dart SLF	Plaxton Pointer 2
	15	DAF SB120	Wright Cadet
	58	Volvo B10M	Plaxton Excalibur
	55	Volvo B7R	Plaxton Prima
	1	Volvo B10M	Plaxton Paragon
Canavan, Kilsyth	2	Dennis Dart SLF	Plaxton Pointer 2
Cardiff Bus	35	Dennis Dart SLF	Plaxton Pointer 2
Chambers, Bures	4	Scania N113	Easy Lancs Cityzen
Cheney, Banbury	3	Dennis Dart SLF	Caetano Nimbus
Chester City Transport	7	Dennis Dart SLF	Marshall Capital
	5	Volkswagen LT46	
Chiltern Queens, Woodcote	1	Volvo B6BLE	East Lancs Spryte
Circle Line, York	2	Dennis Dart SLF	Plaxton Pointer 2
CMT Buses, Liverpool	8	Volvo B10BLE	Wright Renown
Connex Bus	29	Dennis Trident	Alexander ALX400
	14	Dennis Dart SLF	Alexander ALX200
Coombs, Weston	1	Scania N113	East Lancs Cityzen
Cumbrae Coaches	1	DAF SB220	Ikarus
Dart, Paisley	2	Dennis Dart SLF	Caetano
Delaine, Bourne	1	Volvo B7TL	East Lancs Vyking
Dennis's, Ashton	3	Dennis Trident	East Lancs Lolyne
Docklands Minibus	1	Dennis Dart SLF	Caetano Compass
DRM, Bromyard	1	Volvo B10BLE	Alexander ALX300
Dublin Bus	185	Volvo B7TL	Alexander ALX400
	20	Volvo B6BLE	Wright Crusader II
	20	Volvo B7LA	Wright Fusion
Dunn-Line	5	Volvo B10M	Plaxton Excalibur
	4	Scania L94	Wright Axcess-Floline
East Yorkshire	21	Dennis Dart SLF	Plaxton Pointer 2
	2	Volvo B7TL	Plaxton President
	2	Dennis Trident	Alexander ALX400
	6	Volvo B10M	Plaxton Expressliner
	10	Volvo B10BLE	Alexander ALX300
Elcock Reisen, Telford	1	Dennis Dart	Plaxton Pointer 2
Epsom Buses	6	Dennis Dart SLF	Alexander ALX200
Felix, Ilkeston	1	Volvo B10BLE	Alexander ALX300
	1	Dennis Dart SLF	Plaxton Pointer 2
Finglands, Manchester	2	Volvo B7TL	Plaxton President
	2	Dennis Trident	Alexander ALX400
First Beeline	9	Dennis Dart SLF	Alexander ALX200
	3	Dennis Dart SLF	Plaxton Pointer 2
First Bradford	45	Volvo B7L	Alexander ALX400
	22	Optare Solo	
First Bristol	16	Dennis Trident	East Lancs Lolyne
First Capital	22	Dennis Trident	Alexander ALX400
First CentreWest	43	Dennis Trident	Plaxton President
	1	Volvo B7TL	East Lancs Vyking
First Eastern Counties	10	Scania L94	Wright Axcess-Floline
First Glasgow	30	Volvo B10BLE	Alexander ALX300
First Hampshire	18	Volvo B7LA	Wright Eclipse Fusion
	15	Volvo B7TL	Alexander ALX400
	15	Volvo B10BLE	Wright Renown
First Leeds	25	Volvo B7L	Alexander ALX400
First Leicester	12	Volvo B7TL	Alexander ALX400
First Manchester	60	Mercedes Citaro	
	22	Scania L94	Wright Axcess-Floline
	19	Volvo B10BLE	Wright Renown
First Midland Red	2	Dennis Dart SLF	Plaxton Pointer 2
First PMT	16	Optare Solo	
	5	Dennis Dart SLF	Alexander ALX200
First Western National	9	Volvo B6BLE	Wright Crusader II
	11	Optare Solo	
Fishwick, Leyland	4	DAF SB120	Wright Cadet
Go-Ahead London	178	Volvo B7TL	Plaxton President
	46	Volvo B7TL	Alexander ALX400
	17	DAF SB220	East Lancs Myllennium
	13	Dennis Trident	Plaxton President
Go-Ahead North East	27	Dennis Trident	East Lancs Lolyne
	30	Volvo B10BLE	Wright Renown
	37	Dennis Dart SLF	Plaxton Pointer 2
Guide Friday, Stratford	2	Mercedes Citaro	
HAD, Shotts	27	Optare Solo	
Hagvagnar, Iceland	2	Dennis Dart SLF	Plaxton Pointer 2
Halton Transport	6	Dennis Dart SLF	Marshall Capital
Harrogate & District	14	Volvo B6BLE	Wright Crusader II
	4	Volvo B10BLE	Wright Renown
Harte, Greenock	2	Dennis Dart SLF	Plaxton Pointer 2
Hornsby, Scunthorpe	1	Dennis Dart SLF	Plaxton Pointer 2
Hutchison, Overtown	3	Optare Excel	
	2	Volvo B10BLE	Alexander ALX300
Ipswich	12	Dennis Dart SLF	East Lancs Spryte
	3	DAF DB250	Optare Spectra
Isle of Man Transport	11	Dennis Trident	East Lancs Lolyne
	3	DAF DB250	Optare Spectra
Paul James, Coalville	2	Optare Solo	
Johnson, Henley in Arden	2	Mercedes Citaro	
Jones, Wrexham	1	Dennis Dart SLF	Caetano Compass
JP, Middleton	1	Volvo B7TL	East Lancs Vyking
	3	Optare Solo	
K Line, Huddersfield	1	Optare Solo	
Keighley & District	14	Volvo B10BLE	Wright Renown
Kent Coach Tours	1	Volvo B6BLE	East Lancs Spryte
Kettlewell, Retford	2	Scania N113	East Lancs Cityzen
KMB, Hong Kong	129	Volvo Super Olympian	Alex. ALX500 (b)
KMP, Llanberis	1	Dennis Dart SLF	Plaxton Pointer 2
Lakeland, Clitheroe	1	DAF SB220	East Lancs Myllennium
Leon, Finningley	2	Dennis Trident	East Lancs Lolyne
Liverpool City Coaches	1	Dennis Dart SLF	Plaxton Pointer 2

47

Operator	Qty	Model	Body
Lloyd, Bagillt	1	Optare Solo	
Lloyds TSB	1	Dennis Trident	East Lancs Lolyne
London United	45	Volvo B7TL	Alexander ALX400
	26	Volvo B7TL	Plaxton President
London Traveller	4	Volvo B6BLE	East Lancs Spryte
Lothian Buses	6	Volvo B7TL	Plaxton President
	46	Dennis Trident	Plaxton President
	4	Dennis Trident	Plaxton Pres. open-top
	25	Dennis Dart SLF	Plaxton Pointer 2
Ludlow, Halesowen	1	Scania L94	Wright Axcess-Floline
	3	Dennis Dart SLF	Plaxton Pointer 2
	1	DAF SB120	Wright Cadet
Lugg Valley	2	Optare Solo	
Luton Airport	6	DAF SB220	East Lancs Myllennium
Marchwood, Totton	2	DAF DB250	Optare Spectra
Mayne, Manchester	2	Scania N113	East Lancs Cityzen
Metroline	60	Volvo B7TL	Plaxton President
	17	Dennis Trident	Alexander ALX400
	25	Dennis Dart SLF	Plaxton Pointer 2
Mitcham Belle	6	Optare Solo	
MK Metro	6	Optare Solo	
Munro	7	Dennis Dart SLF	Alexander ALX200
National Holidays	10	Volvo B10M	Plaxton Panther
New World First Bus	30	Neoplan Centroliner dd (b)	
Newport Transport	6	Dennis Trident	Alexander ALX400
	5	Dennis Dart SLF	Alexander ALX200
Nottingham City	2	Volvo B12	Plaxton Excalibur
	33	Dennis Trident	East Lancs Lolyne
	68	Optare Solo	
Oban & District	1	Dennis Dart SLF	Plaxton Pointer 2
Oxford Bus Co	6	Volvo B10BLE	Wright Renown
Pandh, Birkenhead	2	Dennis Dart SLF	Caetano Compass
Park, Hamilton	10	Volvo B10M	Plaxton Paragon
Parrys, Cheslyn Hay	11	Neoplan Starliner	
Pete's, West Bromwich	16	Dennis Dart SLF	Plaxton Pointer 2
	6	Dennis Dart SLF	Alexander ALX200
Plymouth Citybus	6	Dennis Dart SLF	Plaxton Pointer 2
Pullman, Crofty	1	Dennis Dart SLF	Alexander ALX200
Preston Bus	11	Dennis Trident	East Lancs Lolyne
Provence Private Hire	2	Scania N113	East Lancs Cityzen
R&B Travel, Ludlow	1	Optare Solo	
Rapson, Inverness	4	Volvo B10M	Plaxton Paragon
	1	Volvo B10BLE	Alexander ALX300
Redwing, London	20	Setra S315	
Reliance, York	1	Volvo B10BLE	Alexander ALX300
Richmond, Barley	4	Mercedes Vario	Plaxton Beaver 2
	1	Optare Solo	
Road Car	5	Dennis Dart SLF	East Lancs Spryte
	6	DAF SB220	East Lancs Myllennium
Rossendale Transport	4	Dennis Dart SLF	Plaxton Pointer 2
Selwyns, Runcorn	1	Dennis Dart SLF	Plaxton Pointer 2
Shamrock, Pontypridd	7	Dennis Dart SLF	Caetano Compass
	5	Optare MetroRider 4	
	3	Scania N113	East Lancs Cityzen
Shearings	10	Volvo B10M	Plaxton Panther
Shire, St Albans	1	Scania N113	East Lancs Cityzen
South Lancs	2	Dennis Dart SLF	Plaxton Pointer 2
Sovereign Bus & Coach	12	Dennis Dart SLF	Plaxton Pointer 2
	10	Volvo B10BLE	Wright Renown
Stockton Borough Council	2	Optare Excel	
Stuart, Carluke	2	Dennis Dart	Plaxton Pointer 2
Jim Stones, Glazebury	4	Dennis Dart SLF	Plaxton Pointer 2
Tayside Transport	12	Volvo B10BLE	Wright Renown (a)
Tellings Golden Miller	21	Dennis Dart SLF	Plaxton Pointer 2
	7	Volvo B10BLE	Alexander ALX300
Thamesdown Transport	5	Dennis Dart SLF	Plaxton Pointer 2
Thornes, Bubwith	1	DAF SB220	East Lancs Myllenni…
Thorpe, London	14	Dennis Dart SLF	Plaxton Pointer 2
TIBS, Singapore	20	Dennis Lance	Metsec
Top Line, York	2	Dennis Dart SLF	Plaxton Pointer 2
Translink	90	Volvo B10BLE	Wright Renown (a)
	6	Mercedes O405N	
	4	Mercedes O405GN artic	
	4	Dennis Dart SLF	Wright
	10	Optare Solo	
Travel West Midlands	102	Volvo B7TL	Plaxton President (a)
Trent	36	Optare Excel	
	28	Optare Solo	
UK North, Manchester	3	DAF SB220	Ikarus
University Bus, Hatfield	3	DAF SB120	Wright Cadet
Wallace Arnold	51	Volvo	Plaxton
Warrington Transport	10	Dennis Dart SLF	Marshall Capital
Weardale	2	DAF SB220	Ikarus
Weavaway, Newbury	2	Scania N113	East Lancs Cityzen
White Rose, Egham	1	Dennis Dart SLF	Caetano Compass
	1	Dennis Dart SLF	Caetano Nimbus
White Star, Brough	4	Dennis Dart SLF	Plaxton Pointer 2
	1	Dennis Dart SLF	Alexander ALX200
Whitelaw, Stonehouse	3	Volvo B6BLE	Wright Crusader II
Whittle, Kidderminster	2	Dennis Dart SLF	Plaxton Pointer 2
Glyn Williams, Blackwood	2	Dennis Dart SLF	Caetano Nimbus
Wilts & Dorset	8	Optare Excel 2	
	6	DAF DB250	Optare Spectra
Wings, London	4	Dennis Dart SLF	East Lancs Spryte
Yeomans	1	Optare Excel 2	
Yorkshire Coastliner	7	Volvo Olympian	Alexander Royale
Yorkshire Terrier	11	DAF SB220	East Lancs Myllenni…
Yorkshire Traction	1	Mercedes O404	Hispano
	12	Volvo B6BLE	East Lancs Spryte
Zaks, Birmingham	2	Optare Solo	

(a) delivered 1999-2000
(b) delivered 2000-2001

Forward orders

Orders announced in 2000 for delivery in 2001 included:

Operator	Qty	Model	Body
AirCoach, Dublin	30	Volvo B10M	Caetano Enigma
Airlinks	12	Mercedes Vario	Plaxton Cheetah
Bebbs	16	Volvo B10M	Plaxton
Bus Eireann	38	Scania	Irizar Century
	15	Volvo B10M	Caetano Enigma
City Trafik, Copenhagen	22	Volvo B7L	East Lancs dd
Delaine, Bourne	1	Volvo B7TL	East Lancs Vyking
Durham Travel	20	Volvo B7TL	Plaxton President
Flights, Birmingham	26	Volvo B10M	Plaxton Panther
Go-Ahead London	42	Volvo B7TL	Plaxton President
	61	Dennis Dart SLF	Plaxton Pointer 2
Hallmark	13	Dennis R	Plaxton Panther
Hams Travel, Kent	1	Volvo B7TL	East Lancs Vyking
National Holidays	10	Volvo B10M	Plaxton Panther
Stagecoach 2001	184	Dennis Trident	Alexander ALX400
	102	Dennis Dart SLF	Alexander ALX200
	50	MAN	Alexander ALX300
Translink	35	Scania L94	Wright Solar
	20	Volvo B7TL	Alexander ALX400
Wallace Arnold 2001	25	Volvo B10M	Plaxton Paragon
	25	Volvo B10M	Jonckheere Mistral 4
Yellow Buses	8	Volvo B7TL	East Lancs Vyking
Yorkshire Coastliner	1	Volvo B10BLE	Wright Renown